PALMISTRY FOR HAPPINESS

"Can your palm predict your future? Can your behavior change the map of your palm? Ghanshyam Singh Birla and Guylaine Vallée take on these questions and more in this thought-provoking look at the predictive art and ancient history of Vedic palmistry. It's a fascinating, fun, and enlightening read!"

THOM HARTMANN, AUTHOR OF *ADHD* AND
ADHD AND THE EDISON GENE

"As a Vedic astrologer, healer, and a graduate of the Birla Center's course in Vedic palmistry, the most important thing I have learned is that no matter what tendencies we have, we need not be influenced by them throughout our lives because we have the free will to change! In this profoundly brilliant and inspiring book, Ghanshyam Singh Birla and Guylaine Vallée teach us this: Our palms show us what we need to change in our life to find happiness. When we make those changes, the lines on our hands will change. This book teaches not only the basics of Vedic palmistry but also specific techniques for making these changes."

JULIANA SWANSON, RN, PALMIST-ASTROLOGER AND
DEAN OF ACADEMICS OF THE AMERICAN COLLEGE
OF VEDIC ASTROLOGY

"Ghanshyam Singh Birla and Guylaine Vallée show us that, like the stars at our birth, our own hands can give us deep insight into our own nature, what we are manifesting of our high soul potential, and, most important, how to expand into that potential to find the highest happiness. Clear and accessible, I recommend *Palmistry for Happiness* to anyone."

JOSEPH SELBIE, AUTHOR OF *THE PHYSICS OF GOD*
AND *THE PHYSICS OF MIRACULOUS HEALING*

"With a profound understanding of the root cause and manifestation of happiness, this book is a literary masterpiece. Ghanshyam Singh Birla and Guylaine Vallée are exemplary in their skills, utilizing ancient wisdom embodied in palmistry to highlight the most treasured trait in life—happiness."

ZIDE MOONI, OMD, ND, FOUNDING DIRECTOR OF
EVOLV WELLNESS AND INTEGRATIVE MEDICINE

Palmistry for Happiness is written with clarity for students and professional practitioners alike. I predict that this book will be a solid cornerstone for any Vedic sciences library."

DENNIS M. HARNESS, PHD, PROFESSOR EMERITUS AT
THE AMERICAN COLLEGE OF VEDIC ASTROLOGY AND
AUTHOR OF THE NAKSHATRAS

PALMISTRY FOR HAPPINESS

The Transformational Power
of Vedic Hand Reading

A Sacred Planet Book

Ghanshyam Singh Birla and Guylaine Vallée

with Steve Erwin

Destiny Books
Rochester, Vermont

Destiny Books
One Park Street
Rochester, Vermont 05767
www.DestinyBooks.com

SUSTAINABLE FORESTRY INITIATIVE — Certified Sourcing
www.forests.org
SFI-00854

Text stock is SFI certified

Destiny Books is a division of Inner Traditions International

Sacred Planet Books are curated by Richard Grossinger, Inner Traditions editorial board member and cofounder and former publisher of North Atlantic Books. The Sacred Planet collection, published under the umbrella of the Inner Traditions family of imprints, includes works on the themes of consciousness, cosmology, alternative medicine, dreams, climate, permaculture, alchemy, shamanic studies, oracles, astrology, crystals, hyperobjects, locutions, and subtle bodies.

Cataloging-in-Publication Data for this title is available from the Library of Congress

ISBN 979-8-88850-037-8 (print)
ISBN 979-8-88850-038-5 (ebook)

Printed and bound in the United States by Lake Book Manufacturing, LLC
The text stock is SFI certified. The Sustainable Forestry Initiative® program promotes sustainable forest management.

10 9 8 7 6 5 4 3 2 1

Text design by Virginia Scott Bowman and layout by Debbie Glogover
This book was typeset in Garamond Premier Pro with Gill Sans MT Pro,
ITC Legacy Sans Std, Myriad Pro, Nexa, and Raleway used as display typefaces

Fig. 4.6 courtesy of Wikimedia Commons (CC BY 2.0) via Flickr: JLA974, Audebaud Jean Louis from Casablanca
Fig. 8.10 © Juliette Powell and Birla Vedic International
Fig. 8.18 courtesy of Wikimedia Commons (CC BY-SA 3.0), photo by Håkan Dahlström

To send correspondence to the authors of this book, mail a first-class letter c/o Inner Traditions • Bear & Company, One Park Street, Rochester, VT 05767, and we will forward the communication, or contact the Birla Vedic Center at **birla.ca**

Scan the QR code and save 25% at InnerTraditions.com.
Browse over 2,000 titles on spirituality, the occult, ancient mysteries, new science, holistic health, and natural medicine.

To all those seeking
self-understanding and happiness
through Vedic palmistry

Contents

Foreword

Joni Patry

Happiness is something we all want and spend most of our lives searching for, but it can also be the hardest thing in the world to find. That's because many of us simply don't know what will make us truly happy and end up chasing joy through material pursuits or in unhealthy ways that inevitably leave us feeling unsatisfied and empty. Real happiness, the kind that brings joy to our lives, our relationships, and our careers, is an inside job—it comes from within.

That's why it is such a pleasure for me to write a few words of introduction for *Palmistry for Happiness: The Transformational Power of Vedic Hand Reading*, by Vedic palmists Ghanshyam Singh Birla and Guylaine Vallée. This wonderful little book is overflowing with insight, wisdom, and practical palmistry techniques that will guide you toward joy and help you find the lasting happiness we are all meant to enjoy in this lifetime.

As a Vedic astrologer, I find Vedic palmistry fascinating. Astrology and palmistry are both divine sciences that come to us through the Vedas, India's most ancient and sacred texts. In fact, Vedic astrology and palmistry are often referred to as sister sciences. The Sanskrit word for astrology is *jyotish*, which describes the light of the planets. The Sanskrit phrase for palmistry combines *jyotish* with the word *hast*, which means "hand." So Vedic palmistry is known as *hast jyotish*—the light of the planets reflected in our hands.

All of our life experiences are etched into our palms, so Vedic palmistry not only helps us understand our past and present but also how to use that knowledge to shape the future we dream of. It is so perfect that the Divine Intelligence would, of course, place a living road map in such an obvious place, allowing us to refer to it for guidance simply by looking into the palm of our hands. This is genius—especially because that map can lead us to inner happiness and joy!

It is truly astounding that the energy of the planets is so perfectly reflected in the lines of the hand. Vedic palmistry perfectly illustrates the ancient axiom "As above, so below" and is a beautiful example of how everything in our universe is interrelated and all things are connected. This echoes the ancient teachings of the Upanishads as well as those of the Greeks, which both urge us to "know thyself." In other words, by understanding ourselves we understand the universe and our place in it. Self-knowledge makes us whole and complete because it not only resides within us but is also reflected in the external world. The Vedic sciences of astrology and palmistry teach this inner reflection and help us to truly know ourselves.

Ghanshyam and Guylaine so eloquently display the Vedic wisdom of palmistry in such a beautiful way that it inspires us to seek out and embrace the simple, universal truth of life—that we have been put in this world to find happiness. In *Palmistry for Happiness* these extraordinary palmists explain that the palm not only teaches us how to interpret our life map but also provides us with the wisdom and methodology to embrace the inner joy that will change our life forever—changes that will register in our hands.

What many people are unaware of is when you change your outlook and attitude, the lines in your hand will also change, reflecting your personal growth and increasing joy. And because your lines reveal your entire life, from your first breath up to the present moment, your palms provide all you need to know to heal past hurts and achieve happiness. When used together, jyotish and hast jyotish have all the answers you need to find joy!

This is brought home to us through the many real-life examples throughout these pages, including before and after handprints that brilliantly illustrate how the lives of individuals have been completely transformed through palmistry.

Best of all, Ghanshyam and Guylaine show us that our search for happiness is really a search for spiritual truth, which we discover through love. Love is the essence of joy and happiness. And, as with the search for truth, the search for love must always start within us. If we are not trusting, then we attract untrustworthy people; if we are suspicious or jealous, then we attract suspicious and jealous people into our lives; and if we are unloving we attract unloving people. This is the law of attraction! But if we learn to put our suspicions aside and practice being trusting and loving, we will attract loving people into our lives. As Ghanshyam and Guylaine explain, we develop this powerful magnetism by looking inward and transforming the lines of our hands—which will inevitably result in positive changes in our lives and in ourselves.

I do not exaggerate when I say that the truths and wisdom found in this beautifully written book will put you on the road to ultimate joy and happiness by helping you to know yourself better. It conveys the universal laws of humanity and imparts the Vedic wisdom that has been passed down through the ages. Like astrology, by practicing the divine science of palmistry we can reach self-realization, which is God consciousness or enlightenment, and with that knowledge comes true wisdom and happiness.

On a personal note, I first met Ghanshyam and Guylaine in the autumn of 2017 when I was invited to the Birla Center to speak on Vedic astrology. That visit is a beautiful and sentimental memory that I cherish. Looking back, it feels like a dream. The center itself was magnificent—located on a quiet lake in Quebec ringed by low-lying mountains and surrounded by trees ablaze in dazzling fall colors! Most of my speaking engagements are generally very businesslike and include a stay at a stuffy hotel where I meet very nice and interesting people, give my lecture, and fly home. However, I always feel a certain sense of judgment since I am teaching Vedic astrology to those who practice Western astrology in a Western culture.

But this visit was unlike any of the others. The warmth and kindness my husband, Daniel, and I were greeted with by the center's small staff were just as beautiful and overwhelming as the gorgeous, serene setting. When we met Ghanshyam and Guylaine, the brilliance and authenticity of their smiles exuded pure joy and happiness. The hospitality was so welcoming and warm, I felt as though I had known them for years;

I had a sense of returning home. Everyone at the Birla Center exuded genuine warmth, love, and a deep appreciation for us. That was as moving to me as it was memorable.

I can honestly say that these dedicated Vedic palmists live life with joy and happiness; they truly walk their talk. Life and learning should be a joyous experience with no feeling of stuffiness or judgment—just fun and laughter, which is what you get with Ghanshyam and Guylaine.

Ghanshyam, who has helped thousands of people through palmistry since leaving his native India many decades ago, was generous with information. He gave both of us readings and showered us with his kindness and complimentary, autographed copies of his numerous books. His presence is incredibly charismatic while being completely authentic! Truly enlightened and full of joy and happiness, Ghanshyam and Guylaine, who have worked together for nearly forty years, emit a light that is contagious; you can't help but feel inspired in their presence. The community they have created is one of love where everyone cares for and supports each other. It is a little heaven right here on Earth. I feel so lucky, and so grateful, to have been invited to such a beautiful place and to have had such a wonderful experience.

I am now fortunate to have the opportunity to express my appreciation to this kind group of loving, knowledgeable people by recommending that everyone read this valuable book as a means of self-realization. I know it will help so many come to the most important realization in this world, which is finding true happiness and discovering inner joy.

I love these beautiful people and want to thank Ghanshyam for his incredible contribution in fostering spiritual enlightenment in this world. And I want to thank Guylaine for the passion and love that abounds in her work as she continues to promote the words and wisdom of her dear friend, wonderful teacher, and inspired mentor, Ghanshyam Singh Birla.

JONI PATRY lives in Dallas, Texas, and is one of the most recognized teachers and practitioners of Vedic astrology in the world with more than forty years of experience. She has published numerous books and has appeared on national and international television shows.

A keynote speaker for international conferences, Joni also regularly teaches all over the world by invitation in Turkey, India, Austria, England, Italy, Australia, and Canada. Joni has been invited multiple times as a keynote speaker at UAC (United Astrology Conference), ISAR (International Society for Astrological Research), NCGR (National Council for Geocosmic Research), and the Sedona Vedic Conference. She has also established her own Vedic conference in Dallas, Texas: the Future of Astrology.

Joni is the founder of the University of Vedic Astrology, an online school for certification in Vedic astrology, UniversityofVedicAstrology.com. Find her also at her personal website GalacticCenter.org and on her YouTube channel: Joni Patry.

Acknowledgments

It is with a great sense of privilege and joy that we present to you *Palmistry for Happiness: The Transformational Power of Vedic Hand Reading*. We are deeply indebted to all of you who helped us along the way.

First of all, we would like to thank our great friend and well-wisher Mary Stark, who inspired this project and was instrumental in bringing it to the attention of acquisitions editor Richard Grossinger.

As always, we are grateful to Ehud and Vatsala Sperling for publishing this third book with us. And many thanks to the great staff of Inner Traditions, who are always so supportive, including Jon Graham, Kelly Bowen, Courtney Jenkins Mesquita, Erica Robinson, Jeanie Levitan, Jamaica Burns Griffin, Jennie Marx, Aaron Davis, Virginia Scott Bowman, and Debbie Glogover.

It is with much love and gratitude that we thank Vedic astrologer extraordinaire Joni Patry, who so generously wrote the foreword for this book.

Thanks to our writing team—Stephen Erwin, Kathy Keogh, and Johanne Riopel—for their untiring dedication in putting this book together. And thanks to the Birla Center staff—Peter Keogh, Denise Parisé, Jacinthe Côté, Rémi Riverin, Colette Hemlin, and Frédérique Herel—for their unwavering love and support. We are also grateful to Sophie Bisaillon, Kyriakos Patoucheas, Sylvie Cousineau, Adoni Makris, Zide Mooni, Maria Aguilera, Ali Mirkarimi, Natalie Wallace, Natasha Stoynoff, Jeannette Chabot, France Jodoin, and Caroline Wilson, who have always been there for us. And, of course, a shout

out to Leo, whose purrs of encouragement spurred us on through thick and thin.

And last, thanks to our families, friends, students, clients, and well-wishers who supported us along the way, especially those who graciously permitted us to use their handprints in the hope of inspiring others.

Happy Hands Make
for a Happy Life
Meet Ghanshyam Singh Birla

If you have picked up *Palmistry for Happiness*, chances are you're looking for a way to bring more happiness into your life or into the life of a friend or a loved one. If that is the case, which I am pretty sure it is, I have good news—you've come to the right place. Believe it or not, the lines crisscrossing your palms create a map of your life; learning to read that map (which you are about to do) will put you on a path toward lifelong happiness. That's not to say you won't face challenges, hardships, or even heartbreak; pain and sorrow are an inevitable

Fig. 1.1. The lines in your palms are a map of your life,
and learning to read that map is the key to lifelong happiness.

1

part of being alive. But palmistry will show you how to transform suffering and sadness into understanding, acceptance, and compassion—a combination that keeps happiness alive and thriving at the core of your being no matter how many lemons the universe dishes out to you.

That's not a pipe dream; it's a fact. I've been a professional Vedic palmist for more than fifty years and have consulted with literally thousands of clients from every walk of life—from incarcerated criminals to Fortune 500 CEOs and everything in between. Without fail, every man, woman, and child who has traveled to my office or contacted me online has done so for the same basic reason—happiness has either eluded him or her or has disappeared from his or her life completely.

Like many of us, most of those clients placed the blame for their discontentment, absence of joy, or a chronic case of the blues on external circumstances, such as a difficult upbringing, a rocky marriage, an unsatisfying job, their physical appearance, or a lack of money. But, as palmistry teaches, real happiness—the kind that endures across the years—can't be found in what we own, the way we look, or the size of our bank account; lasting happiness is an inside job. And that is where the wonder of the lines and signs of the hand comes into play—and comes to the rescue!

Fig. 1.2. Palmistry teaches happiness that endures across the years.

LOOKING BENEATH THE SURFACE

The real beauty of palmistry is that it opens our eyes and our heart so we can see beyond the surface of existence and connect to the source of all happiness—our innermost self. Socrates, perhaps the most famous philosopher of antiquity, told us that true happiness is only possible with self-knowledge—by understanding and accepting ourselves as we are as individuals, which obviously includes all our thoughts, emotions, desires, fears, dreams, and passions. And, in my humble opinion, Vedic palmistry is one of the best methods of increasing our self-awareness, and hence our level of happiness.

Even more exciting is the fact that the lines in our hand trace the history of our life. Our lines show us the choices and decisions we have made in the past and where those choices and decisions have led us. Hence, we can use that information to forecast where we are headed in life, and, if we don't like the outcome, we can use palmistry to make the necessary course corrections to avoid repeating the same mistakes that have held us back. In some ways, being a palmist is like being a meteorologist—we study historical patterns to predict future trends. So, if we have been rocked by stormy relationships in the past, we can use the knowledge we gain from studying our palm to push those storm clouds away once and for all.

For example, if we have been searching for a soulmate but always end up with Mr. or Ms. Wrong, the lines and signs of our hand can help us remedy our unhappy situation. How? Well, broken lines, for

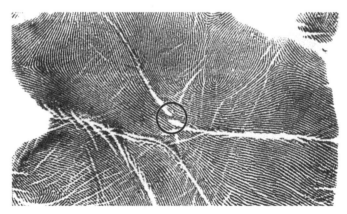

Fig. 1.3. Fixing a broken Heart Line can help heal a broken heart.

instance, often reveal that our issues with other people may actually be unresolved issues we have with ourselves, which we can identify and correct with a basic understanding of our palm. In other words, learning to fix a broken Heart Line could help us heal a broken heart. Indeed, palmistry is a healing science that comes to us from a renowned line of Vedic teaching.

THE FAMILY OF VEDIC SCIENCES

Like yoga, Ayurvedic healing, astronomy, and astrology, Vedic palmistry is founded upon the wisdom and insights of the Vedas, India's most sacred and ancient texts, which are among the earliest written works in history. That doesn't mean the Vedas are a collection of dusty thoughts from the distant past—Vedic math is still taught to millions of students in schools throughout India today, Vedic medicine is practiced throughout the East, and Vedic philosophy is studied in every major university on the planet. But while philosophic and scientific in nature, the Vedas also (and most importantly) provide us with practical advice on living a fulfilling, contented, and *happy* life.

In a nutshell, the Vedas are an incredible compendium of knowledge introduced to the world more than five thousand years ago by Himalayan *rishis* (seers). They provide such a keen window into the human condition that some of the greatest minds of the modern era have been convinced the Vedas are divinely inspired. That includes famed German philosopher Arthur Schopenhauer, renowned writers such as Ralph Waldo Emerson and Henry David Thoreau, Mahatma Gandhi, and physicist Robert Oppenheimer, the father of the atomic bomb, just to name a few.

When it comes to palmistry, the earliest Vedic practitioners realized that the makeup of our palms—every line, sign, and shape—reflected an essential part of our being; that the palm was an uncanny mirror of our mind and a very precise representation of how we think, feel, behave, and use our vital energies.

I discovered that truth a long time ago and with that discovery came the realization that palmistry had the potential to be one of the most effective personal development programs ever devised. Indeed, if you commit to reading this book from start to finish, you will find you

Fig. 1.4. The palm reflects our essential being.

have embarked on an exciting journey of self-discovery that will profoundly enrich your life and fill your heart with happiness, just as it has done for me.

Decades of experience have taught me that Vedic palmistry is a powerful method of examining the most hidden recesses of the human psyche. Studying the handprints of tens of thousands of clients over the years has left no doubt in my mind that our hopes and dreams, phobias and fears, desires and disease, attitudes and addictions are all registered in our hands. More importantly, I have discovered that the root causes for any of these disruptions and distresses in our lives are imbalances in our personal energy, which I refer to throughout this book as *happiness blockers*. These imbalances can be identified, corrected, and even eliminated once we understand what the features of our palms are telling us. Indeed, Vedic palmistry not only promotes positive change, all-around success, and healing and happiness, but it is also a powerful preventive measure we can use to avoid mental, emotional, and physical distress.

HAPPINESS AWAITS
Change Your Lines, Change Your Life

Once again, this is not just a theory, guesswork, or wishful thinking; it is a measurable and quantifiable scientific fact. Why am I so certain that palmistry can change our life for the better? Because the lines of our hands physically change when we consciously change the way we think and behave. Wow! Let me say that again: When we make changes in our attitude, outlook, and actions, we will see changes in the lines of our hands. For example, a short Heart Line can grow into a line that is long and strong when we make a conscious effort to be more loving in word, thought, and deed. Pretty amazing, right? Hence, Vedic palmistry is an extraordinary barometer of personal growth. By taking our handprints at regular intervals, we can witness, monitor, and calculate the progress we are making as we move toward a happier life. In short, Vedic palmistry—which has been practiced with reverence and respect for many centuries in my native India—is a tried-and-true method of establishing, restoring, and maintaining peace of mind and a sense of joy in our lives.

Okay, I've been making some big claims—but if you read on, you will see, as they say, that proof is in the pudding—and in this case the pudding is our handprints. That's why this book includes many before and after handprints from clients whose lives have been transformed through the practice of Vedic palmistry and an understanding of Vedic philosophy, which promotes balance in all things.

MEET THE PALMIST
My Name Is Ghanshyam

But first, if you are committed to joining me on this journey to a happier existence, we'd better get to know each other a bit. I already know that you are a seeker of happiness, but for those of you unfamiliar with my work, let me introduce myself. My name is Ghanshyam Singh Birla, and I am, as mentioned, a professional Vedic palmist. In fact, I have dedicated most of my life to the study, practice, and teaching of Vedic palmistry and helping others use it to solve their problems, reach their goals, and lead more loving, fulfilling, and happier lives.

Following in My Grandfather's Footsteps

My fascination with palmistry began at the knee of my grandfather, whom I affectionately addressed as Dadaji. Grandfather was a gentle, white-bearded, and deeply learned man renowned far beyond the con-

Fig. 1.5. Vedic palmist Ghanshyam Singh Birla

fines of our small village as a great Vedic scholar, palmist, and practitioner of Ayurvedic medicine. I grew up watching him restore wellness, peace of mind, optimism, and even a sense of joy to the hundreds of visitors who knocked on our door seeking his help and sage counsel. He tirelessly tended to their needs in the small courtyard of our home in Northeast India while I stood at his side, paying close attention as he diagnosed patients' problems with uncanny accuracy by analyzing their palms. Most of those who came to see him arrived complaining about life but would leave wearing huge smiles on their faces. I always listened carefully to the remedial advice he offered and felt honored when he occasionally asked for my assistance to dispense the medicinal herbs that he'd spent years cultivating and collecting. His devotion to both his practice and using his knowledge to help others filled me with a lifelong passion to do the same.

Dadaji's wisdom, as they say, was "more precious than rubies," but he never charged for his services. The most valuable lesson he taught me, and there were many, is this: When the energies in our hands are balanced, the energies that create, sustain, and animate our existence will be balanced as well. Balancing our energies is the key to being happy: Balance enables us to think more clearly, love more deeply, overcome adversity more easily, and continually grow healthier in body, mind, and soul regardless of our physical age or circumstances.

Observing my grandfather work with his patients demonstrated to me time and again that restoring and creating balance in our life is a matter of developing self-awareness, which as I have mentioned is one of the main things palmistry helps us to do remarkably well and with surprising speed. Dadaji helped others live happier lives, and in doing so helped make the world a better place in which to live. As I grew older, I became increasingly determined to follow in his footsteps. Indeed, in my early teens—and much to the consternation of my no-nonsense, military officer father—I publicly resolved to devote all my time and energy to learning as much about palmistry, and its relevance to human nature, as possible.

My dad was understandably worried I'd end up as a poor beggar reading palms on a street corner for a few pennies; like all caring fathers, he wanted to see me established in a secure and profitable profession. It is with a twinge of familial guilt that I admit, in defiance of my father's

Fig. 1.6. Ghanshyam (*right*) with his beloved grandfather and his younger sister, Leila

wishes and to follow my passion, I often snuck out of the house when he was asleep to sketch the palms of a willing passerby on the sidewalks of New Delhi. I recorded and studied every palm willingly submitted to me for analysis, including the hands of police officers, prostitutes, and pandits. At home, I poured through the rare Vedic texts and age-old Ayurvedic treatments shelved in my grandfather's extensive library. I also had the good fortune of attending a specialized boarding school (a *gurukul*) that emphasized Vedic education and spent hundreds of hours learning mantra recitation, yogic breathing techniques, and how to meditate more deeply—all of which are wonderful, peace-inducing methods of self-reflection that promote spiritual development and personal happiness. Dadaji introduced all of this to me when I was still practically a toddler, and I will share this with you in the coming chapters.

At the gurukul I mastered Sanskrit, which allowed me to study the Vedic sciences in their original language. This aided me greatly when I moved on to university where I continued to research and practice palmistry. Upon graduation, I accepted a professorship in physical fitness and personal discipline with the federal government, a much-treasured post that took me to schools all across India, affording me the opportunity to study the palms of countless teachers and students from every walk of life. At the same time, I was privileged to come under the private tutelage of the notoriously reclusive Sri Shyamlalji, a profoundly spiritual man well-versed in Vedic wisdom and a highly sought-after palmist. With Shyamlalji's guidance, I expanded my understanding of the spiritual underpinnings of palmistry and how its practice connects us with the divine spark that resides within us all and is the original source of joy. Eventually I gained the knowledge, skill, and loyal clientele needed to open my first palmistry center in the heart of New Delhi. I managed to grow the center into a bustling hub of Vedic learning while keeping up with my rigorous daily meditation routine, private consultations, and teaching duties.

After another decade of study and practice, I followed my heart's desire (and what I'd come to believe was my purpose in life) to share all I'd learned about Vedic palmistry with people who had never heard of this incredible science—which meant leaving India and venturing into the wider world. So I resigned from my professorship, closed my beloved center, and moved to Canada to introduce this life-changing form of palmistry to the West. I confess, I arrived in that strange and snowy new land with four dollars in my pocket, but my faith and conviction in my mission energized me and helped me prevail; within a couple of years, I founded the Birla College and was soon consulting with clients all over North America. Today, together with a small but dedicated team of personally trained Vedic palmists, we continue to offer online consultations, courses, and self-development programs in palmistry.

One of my students, Guylaine Vallée, my star pupil and colleague for the past forty years and coauthor of this book, is a living example of the power of Vedic palmistry. She has happily volunteered to provide you with her own story about how palmistry transformed her chronic despondency and depression into happiness and a joy-filled life. She will share with you everything she has learned over the past four decades. I know you are going to love her and be inspired by her work. You will be hearing a great deal from her quite shortly.

As for me, I am and shall forever remain motivated by the unshakable belief that by understanding what our hands reveal about our nature—and letting our thoughts and deeds be governed by that enormous storehouse of self-knowledge—palmistry can and will balance our

Fig. 1.7. Ghanshyam and Guylaine

energies, improve our lives, and increase our level of happiness immeasurably. Indeed, the results speak for themselves, as you will personally witness in all the "before and after" handprints contained in this text.

What We Do at the Birla Center to Create Happiness

When clients contact us with serious problems that are blocking them from being happy—perhaps a contentious divorce, a perturbing health issue, a parenting difficulty, a career dilemma, or a combative work relationship—we use palmistry to assess how harmoniously they are using their energies. We then identify the underlying cause of any energy imbalances that exist. As Aristotle—a famous philosopher in the line of Socrates and Plato—once said: "Knowing yourself is the beginning of all wisdom." Understanding the imbalances seen in our hand and realizing we are the creators of the behavioral patterns blocking our path to happiness gives us the power to change our thoughts and restore harmony to our lives. And learning to live a balanced life is the only surefire recipe for a happy existence. The lessons you will learn in this book will provide you with concrete and practical steps—such as yoga, meditation, active introspection, and the ancient breathing technique of *pranayama*—that you can employ to restore balance to your life. Harmonizing your energies creates a synergy between mind, body, and soul that produces clarity of thought and intention, a vigorous strength of body, and purity of heart. These multiple blessings in turn generate a strong personal magnetism, attracting positive circumstances and supportive, encouraging people to enter your life.

But please don't think I am suggesting palmistry is some sort of magic wand that makes your problems suddenly disappear. There is nothing magical about Vedic palmistry; as I've stated, it is a precise scientific tool that will radically transform your life.

However, it is ultimately up to you to initiate that positive change by using palmistry to learn all you can about yourself and discover your true identity—who you really are at the core of your being and the reason you were put on this Earth. When you accomplish that, you can accomplish just about anything, including shaping your own unique destiny, fulfilling your dreams, and finding happiness in all you do.

At the Birla College, our approach to palmistry reflects one simple truth: The journey to happiness begins in our hands. Hopefully,

Fig. 1.8. Practicing pranayama restores balance.

Palmistry for Happiness may prove to be your first step on that journey; it is a path that leads to the joyful and peace-filled life we all desire.

I OFFER YOU MY HANDS

But I don't want you to take what I say on face value. I practice what I preach, so I offer my own handprints for you to study—both as a source of inspiration and as living proof of palmistry's power to transform stress, anxiety, and unhappiness into a calm and peaceful state of joy.

My before handprints were taken shortly after arriving in North America to begin a job as a palmist in a Montreal restaurant. I know that sounds like a humble beginning for a mission intended to improve the world through palmistry, and it was, but my hope was to establish myself and open a palmistry school as soon as possible. It was a highly stressful time for me as I had left my wife and two young children—one still in diapers—back in India with the promise I would bring them over as soon as I had enough money. The problem was the wage at the restaurant was barely enough to cover one meal a day and to rent a tiny room in a dilapidated, overcrowded boarding house.

I was worried sick about my family and what the future was going to bring. To say my mind was not at peace would be an understatement—I was totally stressed-out. Indeed, my deep level of anxiety is clearly evident in the network of fine, fragile interference lines crisscrossing my palm. Interference lines, as we will discover in the coming chapters, are major happiness blockers and signs of poor physical, mental, or spiritual well-being—and sometimes all three at once.

A heavy presence of interference lines, the kind seen in my handprints, denotes a compromised immune system, and, indeed, I soon contracted double pneumonia and fell gravely ill. On top of that, because I was too sick to work, I faced the constant threat of deportation. My dream of transforming the world through palmistry was about to evaporate, and I feared I would be shipped back to New Delhi as a failure, both penniless and unemployed.

Fortunately, an acquaintance I made at the restaurant came to visit me as I lay sick and despondent and handed me a bowl of chicken soup along with a copy of *Autobiography of a Yogi*, the international bestseller by Paramahansa Yogananda, an enlightened guru whom you'll be hearing a lot about in these pages. Well, to make a long story short, the soup nourished my body, but that incredible book nourished my spirit by introducing me to a regenerative form of yoga known as Kriya and by reminding me about the transformative power of daily meditation and self-reflection. Indeed, Paramahansa's wisdom helped me realize I had lost my balance; I was letting my fears get the better of me. Most importantly, meditation helped me to look beyond my personal concerns and inspired me to connect to my highest self—the level of consciousness through which we can become attuned to the whispers of our soul.

I began meditating each day and reflecting on what was truly important to me, which was taking care of my family and sharing the wonders of Vedic palmistry with others. In a matter of weeks, I was fully rejuvenated in body and soul; I was back on my feet and back at work. As my energy returned, my heart began filling with joy. I had reconnected with my purpose in life and each morning I rededicated myself to fulfilling my mission.

Fig. 1.9. Paramahansa Yogananda

When my after handprints were taken a few months later, there wasn't a trace of fear or anxiety to be found. As you can see for yourself, all the interference lines that were covering my palm and blocking my happiness completely disappeared. Even better, because I was radiating both joy and my deep love of palmistry, I attracted supportive friends into my life who wanted to see me succeed. Soon I had both the funding and the space to open the Birla Center, build my college, and bring my family to Canada. I had never been happier, and that happiness has stayed with me for the past five decades. My deepest hope is that this book helps you to use palmistry to find the same type of lasting happiness that I have been blessed with.

And while we've tried to make *Palmistry for Happiness* as fun and user-friendly as possible, I did not take on this project lightly. This book is the culmination of my fifty-plus years of research, counseling, and teaching—it is my life's work. I am delighted that you have expressed

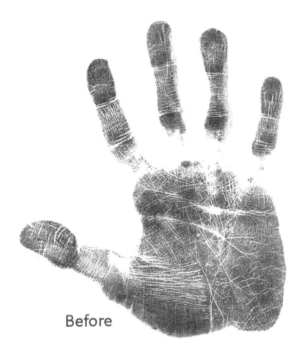

Before

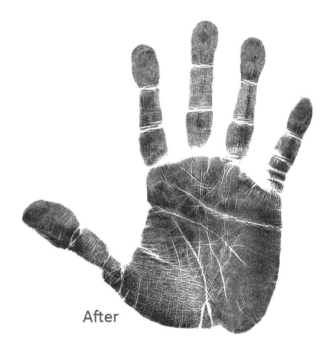

After

Fig. 1.10. My before handprints are filled with interference lines,
which have disappeared in my after handprints.

an interest in learning how the ancient science of Vedic palmistry can help bring happiness and harmony into your life, and I am determined to help you succeed in doing just that. I must confess I am a little selfish in this regard because your happiness is my happiness. So enjoy the journey—you will be a healthier, more balanced, and vastly happier person long before it's over.

The Happy Palmist

Introducing Guylaine Vallée

I am truly overjoyed that you've decided to pick up *Palmistry for Happiness*—our little book that will change your life in a very big way. In fact, what you are about to learn in these pages will not only put a smile on your face but is certain to put you on the path toward deep and lasting happiness, a path that has filled my life with joy for more than forty years! I'm not saying I haven't faced struggle, hardships, and heartache in my life—but no matter how tough things have gotten, the profound sense of happiness radiating at the core of my being has never been extinguished; it carries me through even my most challenging trials and tribulations and ensures that song in my heart is never silent for long.

There is nothing unique or even particularly special about me. I am just an average person with normal problems—but I wake up just about every morning with a smile on my face, eager to jump out of bed and see what new happiness the day will bring. The same holds true for many of my friends and clients. What's the secret? Well, we will get to that in the coming chapters as I share the stories (and handprints) of some of the happiest people I know. But first, allow me to introduce myself and tell you about the event that lifted me out of a miserably depressed state of mind by opening my eyes to the powerful and permanent source of inner happiness that dwells within us all.

Now, some of you have known me for years, either as a friend, a client, or both—which is usually the case! Others have gotten to know

Fig. 2.1. Meet Guylaine.

me through my books and the Birla Center programs I host. These include my memoir, *The Happy Palmist: My Joyful Adventure in Vedic Palmistry*, as well as our online self-development palmistry programs, such as the 90-day challenges for the Heart Line, Head Line, and Life Line—all of which have received scores of accolades and overwhelmingly positive reviews. I am truly grateful to have been of service and deeply humbled by the generous feedback readers have provided—I cherish your kind words!

However, there are undoubtedly quite a few of you that will be getting to know me for the first time in *Palmistry for Happiness*, so I'd like to take a moment to share a little pertinent information about myself and my coauthor, Ghanshyam Singh Birla. Hopefully this will make your reading experience more intimate, meaningful, fun, and effective! Besides, I love making new friends—you can never have enough!

So please, allow me to introduce myself. My name is Guylaine Vallée and I grew up in a small town in rural Quebec, the youngest kid in a large and loving working-class family. Like a lot of young people, however, I lacked purpose and direction in life. Most teenagers grow out of this—I didn't. I carried around a pretty constant depression throughout my teens, and my lack of purpose haunted me well into my twenties. Despite a supportive and caring family, getting a good education, and finding a great job working in television production (my dream career) in Paris (my dream city), I was never happy and always felt something was missing. On the outside it seemed that I had it all, but on the inside I was secretly miserable.

Then one day in the mid-1980s the universe directed me to the Birla Center in Montreal, where I had a consultation with Ghanshyam. I recount every detail of that meeting in my memoir, which was easy to do because even forty-plus years later I remember it as though it happened yesterday. I was back in Montreal and overheard some people talking about visiting an Indian palmist who had completely changed their lives in just a few short sessions. Even though I was drained of both energy and optimism, I jotted down the name of the place and booked myself a session.

Fig. 2.2. Lost and lonely in Montreal

On the morning of my appointment, I woke up with more excitement and enthusiasm than I had felt in months. Could this be the day that my unhappiness finally lifted and I rediscovered some passion for life? As always, I didn't want anyone to see my inner sadness, so I tried to hide it by dressing in my most colorful clothes from Paris, including my electric blue leather pants that went so well with my bleached, asymmetrical pixie haircut. My outfit's pièce de résistance was a transparent plastic purse with a huge plastic fish inside—a one-of-a-kind Paris original!

The Birla Center was across town in the Montreal neighborhood of Westmount, and during the long ride on the number 24 bus I thought of questions to ask the palmist, all of which I forgot the moment I arrived at the Center for hast jyotish.

When I opened the door, an alarm chimed with the sound of songbirds, whose sweet singing followed me up the stairs into the reception area, fragrant with the soothing aroma of burning incense. I felt as though I had just climbed up to heaven.

A woman with long, black hair met me in the lobby and led me to a sink, where she used a little rubber paint roller to coat my hands with black ink. She then pressed each of my palms onto a sheet of blank, white paper. And there they were: my handprints. I had no way of knowing that I was looking at my two new best friends—friends that held the secrets of my past, the path to my future, and the key to unlock them both. When I saw my prints for the first time, I was shocked at how long my fingers were and how big my hands looked. I felt a little exposed, knowing that my hands—and all they might reveal about me—would soon be scrutinized by the eyes of an expert.

"We'll be ready for you in a jiffy, Guylaine," the receptionist said.

This is it, the moment of truth, I thought.

THE MAN IN THE GOLDEN SLIPPERS

I washed the ink from my hands and sat down to wait for my reading. A few minutes later, Ghanshyam walked into the room. I was struck by how dignified he looked in his beige Nehru suit—while wearing a pair of hand-knitted golden slippers! I was amazed someone could be confident and comfortable wearing slippers to work. He had a thin, black moustache and penetrating brown eyes that lit up like birthday candles as he welcomed me with a warm smile.

Oh my! He looks even more beautiful than before, I thought, feeling a powerful surge of déjà vu. *Guylaine, don't be silly! This is the first time you've ever seen him!*

"Hello, hello, helloooo! It is so nice to meet you!" Ghanshyam said in a sweet, lilting East Indian accent. He took my hands in his and shook them with such genuine affection—it felt like a reunion with a long-lost friend. He radiated with an honest-to-goodness kindness that put me instantly at ease.

"Please, come with me, my dear."

I followed him into his office, which was dominated by an armoire filled with books about palmistry and astrology, many of them worn by age and use, bearing titles in languages I did not recognize. A large portrait of an Indian man wearing an orange robe hung above Ghanshyam's desk. The man's face was serene and his eyes were half-shut in a trance-like state. His arms were raised with open palms, as though he were bestowing a blessing upon me while I took my seat.

Fig. 2.3. Ghanshyam in his office library

A young female translator joined us for the session as Ghanshyam spoke no French and, back then, the extent of my English was limited to "How are you today?" She informed me that Ghanshyam practiced Vedic palmistry, a form of traditional Indian palmistry that originated in the ancient Hindu scriptures known as the Vedas.

He placed the paper with my handprints on the desk, next to my astrological chart, which he had drawn up before my arrival. I had been unaware that astrology was related to palmistry, but I learned they are twin sciences and that *hast jyotish* is a phrase combining two Sanskrit words—*hast*, meaning "hand," and *jyotish*, meaning "light." So *hast jyotish* describes the light from our planets being reflected in our hands.

After studying my chart and making all sorts of notes and scribbles on my prints with various colored pens, Ghanshyam looked up at me. His brown eyes shone with such intensity I felt he was staring into my soul.

"Let's begin, shall we?" His voice had the tone of a compassionate doctor who had examined a patient's X-rays and had both good and bad news to deliver.

"You are on a mission to find God and you have been on this quest for a long time," he said, "but you haven't made a spiritual connection. You're miserable because you are stuck in one place and have no direction, which has made you feel lost, alone, and very unhappy. You can't decide what to do, and that has left you without any meaning or purpose in your life. Does that sound right to you?"

I was too overwhelmed to speak. He knew exactly what I had been feeling for the past decade—as if he had known me my entire life. I nodded.

Ghanshyam looked down at my prints and began pointing to various lines with his pen.

"Look here. Your Destiny Line is fragmented, your Sun Line is barely existent, your thumb lacks distance from your Jupiter finger, and your Mount of Jupiter is depleted and your Venus lacks balance."

I was lost in the details, not understanding a word of the technical aspects of palmistry. I did not know at the time that we all have a dominant hand (the one we write with) that reveals our present; it denotes where we currently are in our life and what we want to achieve. And we have a nondominant hand that reflects our past; it shows the tendencies that we have brought with us into this life.

And who knew that the way we hold our thumbs reveals our level of willpower and self-confidence? The flood of data was dizzying, but when Ghanshyam finished his initial analysis his conclusions were painfully accurate.

"You have twelve flaws that are blocking you—they are undermining your spiritual growth and making your destiny unclear. You feel uncomfortable in the world and have closed yourself off—and that is making you unhappy . . . very unhappy."

Then, in quick succession, he wrote down ten of the flaws on my handprint sheet, quickly filling in the white space between the dark, inky images of my two palms. It was a very disconcerting list.

- No decision
- No willpower
- No direction
- No discipline
- No motivation
- No inspiration
- No one point of view or single-mindedness
- No meditation
- No exercise
- No intellectual and/or spiritual work, which will give you hope, trust, joy, faith, and a sense of identity

Ghanshyam's pen hovered for a moment and then, at the top of the page, he added what he said were the two greatest flaws of all: no faith in myself and no self-confidence.

"You have a good Head Line that reflects great intelligence, so I'm sure you will eventually find success in your career. But, he said, shaking his head, "you will probably continue to be unhappy and feel the same sense of emptiness."

He tapped his pen against my print, pointing to the center of my palm.

"Your Destiny Line suggests you could find something that gives you happiness, but not until your early forties."

Oh my God, I thought, *I have to live like this for another twenty years?* I could not imagine the misery of such a long, unhappy life.

Tears were streaming down my face. Ghanshyam, who had been very calm and respectful throughout the reading, slid a box of tissues toward me.

"Don't be upset, the lines on our hands aren't carved in stone—this isn't fortune-telling. Our palms show us what we need to change in our life to find happiness. When we make those changes, the lines on our hands will change. Palmistry is about personal growth!" he said with that same smile he had greeted me with.

"But my question for you, Guylaine, is this: Do you want to change, or do you want to stay like you are? Do you want to make a choice right now to be happy?"

"I want to change, Ghanshyam," I sobbed. "I want to be happy—I choose to be happy."

"Gooooood! Then you will change . . . and you will be happy!" he announced with total delight, throwing his arms open and letting out a booming, hearty laugh. "You've chosen to be happy, and that makes all the difference!"

He fixed his gaze upon me again, disappearing into his own thoughts for a few moments. Then he returned to my sheet with his pen and wrote "12 MONTHS" above my handprints.

"You have a mission in life; you will be of service to many people. But your mission won't begin for another year, not until you're ready."

My heart was pounding so hard, all I could hear for a few seconds was a steady thud, thud, thudding in my ears. Then, all I heard was the echo of his words: "You have a mission in life; you will be of service to many people."

Ghanshyam's words were a healing balm for my aching soul. He suggested steps I could take to "open myself up" and prepare for what life had in store for me. He explained that certain breathing techniques would correct imbalances in my body's energy system, and he suggested that I read *Autobiography of a Yogi* by Paramahansa Yogananda who brought yoga to the West from India in the 1920s. Ghanshyam pointed to the picture of the man in the orange robe above his desk, who I now felt had been watching over me since I had entered the room.

"Paramahansa's book could help you a great deal," Ghanshyam said. Then he suggested we meet every other week for five more sessions.

"We will devise a program together that will help you to develop trust and confidence in yourself and make the changes you need to

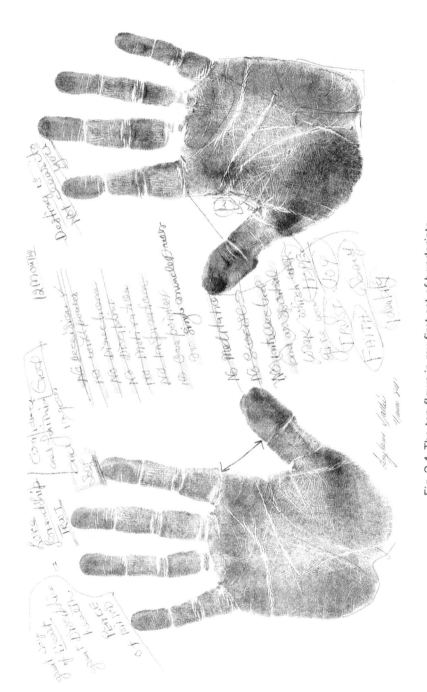

Fig. 2.4. The ten flaws in my first set of handprints

bring great joy into your heart and find peace of mind. And then you'll see, Guylaine—your life will fill up with friendship, trust, and love! And those are the seeds that will grow into lifelong happiness. One day, you will spread those seeds to others and share what you have learned with thousands of souls. How about that!"

Ghanshyam had delved deep into my heart during our hour-long session, and when he walked around the desk to give me one of his enormous hugs that I would come to love, I wanted to jump into his golden slippers. "Don't worry, everything will be fine," he promised.

This man I had never met before, who came from another continent and a different culture, had just touched my heart like no one else had ever done. I was certain that my life was about to change. As I left his office I felt something I hadn't in a long time—I was happy . . .

Well, as they say, the rest is history. Ghanshyam's incredible warmth and knowledge changed the course of my life, and in just one session I learned more about myself than I had in my quarter-century on the planet!

The truth and wisdom of Vedic philosophy, and Vedic palmistry in particular, spoke directly to my heart—it taught me how to be loving and happy even when life was challenging and painful! In fact, palmistry was such a positive force in my life and had so much to offer me, I decided to make it my career. Within a year of my first consultation with Ghanshyam, I was working at the Birla Center full time. Indeed, I have been here ever since—first as a student of Vedic palmistry, then as a palmist, writer, consultant, and webinar host.

LOOK INTO MY HANDS
A Personal Ode to Joy

I am not only a spokesperson for palmistry, I'm a living example of how the lines in our hands can and do change. You can see by comparing my before and after handprints that the entire shape of my palm has transformed, reflecting the huge changes taking place within me. I was slowly conquering the twelve flaws Ghanshyam said were blocking my happiness.

The first thing that Ghanshyam told me to do was to find a sense of purpose. I did that by dedicating myself to the study of palmistry and meditating every day, which helped me to know myself better. By doing this, all the other flaws on Ghanshyam's list—like discipline and focus—naturally took care of themselves.

You can also see in my after prints that my Head Line has grown in length, which shows my vision of the future was more hopeful and I was open to all the possibilities that lay ahead of me. What made me especially happy is that my Heart Line developed three prongs—a sign

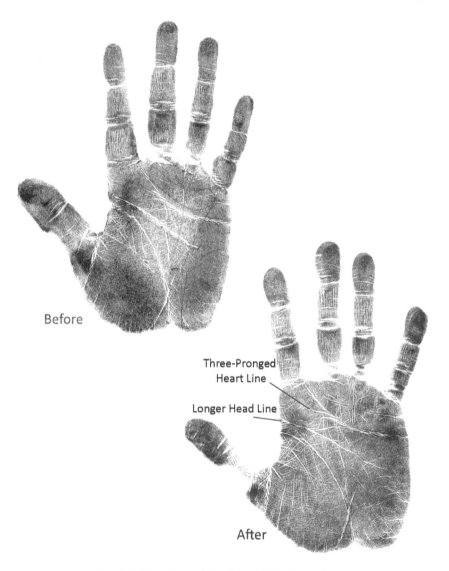

Before

Three-Pronged
Heart Line

Longer Head Line

After

Fig. 2.5. My after prints: A handful of happiness

that I was no longer closing myself off and feeling uncomfortable in the world, but able to express myself more freely. Indeed, my life is a joy and, for that reason, I am happy to share with you my journey so you can be happy, too.

Okay, that's enough about me! Now, let's get to the reason that brought us all here in the first place—tapping into your inner joy and creating a deep and abiding sense of happiness through palmistry! So, if you're ready, let's turn the page and begin our journey by learning the nitty-gritty details of Vedic palmistry and how to apply them to your daily life. We'll start by outlining some of the basics of the hand and then move on to the step-by-step formula for creating happiness, which Ghanshyam, my beloved teacher, mentor, coauthor, and lifelong friend, has taught to me.

The Basics of Vedic Palmistry

Now that you know who we are and what we do at the Birla Center, it's time to get down to the brass tacks of how to use palmistry to create a happier life.

Vedic palmistry is a system of self-inquiry and self-understanding designed to promote a balanced, healthy, and happy lifestyle. It teaches us how to interpret the personal information encoded in our hands so we can identify any energy imbalances blocking us from happiness. Once those issues are identified, we can use the signs and lines of the palm to guide us to adjust our thoughts and attitudes and restore harmony to our body, mind, and heart.

But to successfully use palmistry to free ourselves of happiness-blocking imbalances, we must have a general understanding of the basics of the hand—the major lines, minor lines, and mounts—and how they work together to show us the path to a more joyous life. So let's begin with the ABCs of palmistry.

THE ABCs OF PALMISTRY

The Major Lines, Minor Lines, and Mounts

Palmistry is constructed upon three basic components:

1. The three major lines of Heart, Head, and Life
2. A variety of minor lines, which include the Destiny Line, the Union

(or Marriage) Line, the Love of Truth Line, and the Sun Line, to name a few

3. The ten mounts, the planetary zones of the hand

The goal of palmistry is to ensure the energies in each of the three components are balanced, which denotes overall harmony in our life. Balanced mounts and lines are the building blocks of happiness.

If a line or mount is imbalanced because it is expressing either too much energy (overactive) or too little energy (underactive), those imbalances will show up in our daily lives and lead to discord and unhappiness. Multiple imbalances across the palm suggest we are dealing with problematic issues in many areas of our lives that are blocking us from being happy.

The three components of palmistry—the major and minor lines and mounts—are layered in the palm like sheets of paper stacked one atop the other. The mounts are the first layer, the major lines are in the middle, and the minor lines form the top layer.

We will explore all three components throughout this book, but to provide you with an overview, we will start with a thumbnail sketch of each, beginning with the mounts.

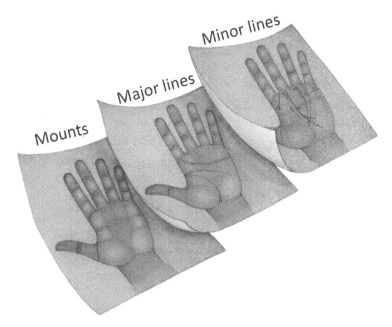

Fig. 3.1. The three basic components of palmistry

A Thumbnail Sketch of the Mounts

The mounts are the ten "planetary zones" of the hand, with each representing the energies, qualities, and characteristics of the planet it is associated with. Furthermore, because the mounts form the foundational layer of the palm, they represent the deepest level of our psyche—our superconscious nature, which is composed of the most deeply held convictions and beliefs that we have developed over numerous lifetimes.

The ten mounts are: the Moon, also known as Luna (☽); Venus (♀); Mars, represented by two mounts—Mars negative (♂-) and Mars positive (♂+); Jupiter (♃); Saturn (♄); Sun (☉); Mercury (☿); Rahu (☊); and Ketu (☋).

The most prominent attribute of each of the ten mounts is as follows: Luna (perception), Venus (love), Mars negative (physical strength), Mars positive (mental stamina), Jupiter (purpose), Saturn (discipline), Sun (magnetism), and Mercury (communication). The mounts of Rahu and Ketu are somewhat unique because they aren't actual heavenly bodies; they are karmic in nature and relate to invisible points of intersection in the orbits of the Earth and the Sun at the vernal and autumnal equinoxes.

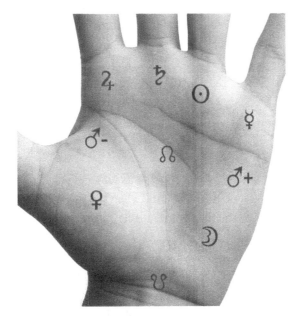

Fig. 3.2. The mounts:
the planetary zones of the hand

Five of the ten mounts have a special significance as they are connected to the five fingers, each of which represent one of the five elements of Creation—Venus (Earth), Jupiter (Water), Saturn (Fire), Sun (Air), and Mercury (Ether). We will explore the significance of the elements in later chapters.

In the hand, Rahu and Ketu represent points of intersection between the other mounts, which means they play a key role in how the mounts interact with one another. Rahu reflects the karma we are creating in the present moment, and Ketu reflects our accumulated past karma.

Harmonious and balanced mounts act like fertile soil in the palm; they ensure the growth of strong and healthy major and minor lines. A line that travels across balanced mounts will be healthier and better nurtured than a line that traverses negatively developed ones.

A Thumbnail Sketch of the Major Lines

Resting on top of the mounts, we find the second (middle) layer of the palm—the three major lines of Heart, Head, and Life. The major lines travel across the mounts and reflect our subconscious nature, which itself represents the way we express our emotions (Heart Line), our thoughts (Head Line), and our physicality (Life Line).

Specifically, the Heart Line denotes our emotional health and our capacity to give and receive love; the Head Line reflects the way we think, which determines both our attitude toward life as well as how we perceive ourselves and the world around us; and the Life Line reflects our overall health and well-being, and our ability to experience what the ancients referred to as *ananda*—the visceral sense of joy everyone can feel simply by being alive.

A Thumbnail Sketch of the Minor Lines

Resting upon the major lines, we find the third (top) layer of the palm, which is composed of the minor lines. The minor lines create a conscious outlet of expression for our subconscious major lines. In other words, the minor lines are the channel through which we express our feelings (Heart Line), our thoughts (Head Line), and our way of living (Life Line).

The minor lines also provide us with a way to express the energy of our superconscious mounts. For example: how objectively we perceive (Luna); how unconditionally we express love (Venus); how productively we expend our physical and mental energy (Mars negative and positive); whether or not we've developed a purpose in life (Jupiter); how disciplined and determined we are (Saturn); the amount of magnetism we exude (Sun); how eloquently we communicate our ideas (Mercury); how successful we are in fulfilling our past karma (Ketu); and our depth of gratitude regarding our present circumstances (Rahu).

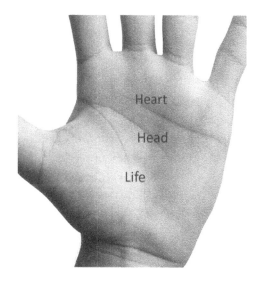

Fig. 3.3. The major lines of Heart, Head, and Life

1. Destiny Line
2. Sun Line
3. Mercury Line
4. Girdle of Venus
5. Ring of Solomon
6. Union Line
7. Interference Line

Fig. 3.4. Minor lines

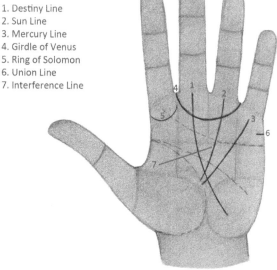

Indeed, the minor lines are a gauge that can instantaneously reveal our state of mind. Examining them gives us an immediate picture of our level of happiness and how satisfied or dissatisfied we are with our life.

The emergence of positive minor lines in the palm reflects both a growing awareness and an increased desire to make the most of our lives. In contrast, negative minor lines (which are signs of obstruction or interference) show that we may be experiencing frustration, anguish, and other nonproductive emotions. Signs of obstruction are warning signals; they indicate that we need to rethink areas of our life and make course corrections to get back on track.

In summary, when the three components of the hand are functioning well individually and are harmoniously integrated with each other, we not only achieve balance in our daily life but also create a pathway in our consciousness through which we can recognize and embrace the eternal aspect of ourselves—our soul nature—and find happiness.

Now that we have a handle on the basic components of the palm, we are ready to take a deeper dive in our superconscious self by exploring the mounts in greater detail.

A DEEP DIVE INTO THE MOUNTS

Our Superconscious Self

In Hindi, the mounts are referred to as *parwat*, which means "little mountains." Indeed, in the hand, the mounts are precisely that—pads of flesh that rise above the palm like miniature mountains; they represent the most elevated aspects of our nature, our superconscious beliefs and convictions.

The mounts indicate the degree to which we are in tune with our superconscious—with the most refined characteristics of our human nature, such as selfless love, compassion, and empathy. When the mounts are balanced, a channel opens within us where we are more capable of hearing or intuiting the intrinsic wisdom of our soul nature.

However, mounts that are not balanced are major happiness blockers that interfere with our ability to recognize and act from our soul nature. For example, the quality of nurturing love associated with our Venus mount could be improperly channeled as jealousy or selfishness if the Mount of Venus is imbalanced. Indeed, imbalanced mounts weigh

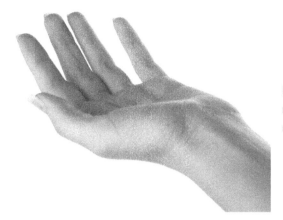

Fig. 3.5. The mounts are referred to as *parwat*—"little mountains."

down our consciousness; the light of our soul is cast in a shadow, confining our awareness to the thoughts and perceptions of our limited mind and the desires of our individualistic egos. Consequently, the lines that travel over imbalanced mounts will reflect personal struggles, ego conflicts, and complications rather than harmony, peace, and happiness.

By understanding the qualities of each mount, we are better equipped to access and develop our superconscious awareness, which will align us with our soul nature—our true and most joyous self. It's up to us to use our free will to direct the energy of the mounts in the most positive, uplifting manner possible through our thoughts, attitudes, and actions. By cultivating an attunement to our superconscious—our link to infinite Spirit—we become free within ourselves. We recognize the unlimited possibilities of soul—existing in a state of peace, love, and joy, unfettered by the limitations of mind.

A balanced mount is a beautiful thing; we are expressing the very best qualities the mount has to offer and resonating with the finest qualities within our human nature. However, imbalanced mounts are often the most challenging happiness blockers we encounter in life. There are two ways a mount can be imbalanced; it is expressing too much energy (overactive) or too little energy (underactive)—either way, an imbalanced mount often spells unhappiness.

Hence, it is imperative for our happiness to develop the most positive qualities within the mounts and learn how to bring an imbalanced mount back into harmony. And the best way to do that is by taking a trip around the palm and spending a little time exploring each

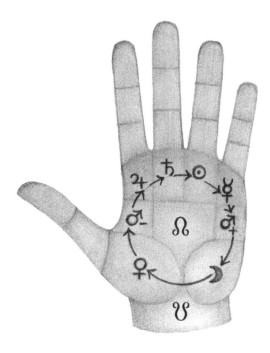

Fig. 3.6. Around the palm:
A tour of the mounts

individual mount. Every stop along the way will provide us with deeper insight into the importance of these superconscious zones of the hand. We will provide you with a general rule for determining the level of balance in each mount. However, it's important to note that the effects of an imbalanced mount can be mitigated by the appearance of wisdom markings on the mount, which we will discuss later in the book.

Okay, we are ready to begin our tour of the mounts; we'll start at the base of the palm, with the Mount of Luna.

The Mount of Luna
**How We Perceive Ourselves, Our Life,
and the World Around Us**

The Mount of Luna governs our five senses of perception—smell, taste, sight, touch, and hearing—which means that Luna pretty much governs the way we see, feel, experience, and interpret everything we encounter in the world. In short, Luna is responsible for our thoughts, which means it affects every single aspect of our lives—from our moods and emotions to our relationships, our self-image, our mental health, and our actions. And given the overwhelming amount of recent mind-body research illustrating the enormous impact our thoughts and emotions have on our bodies Luna also plays a major role in our physical health and well-being. Luna also happens to be the seat of our creativity and imagination. So, if we are looking for happiness, developing a balanced Luna is where we begin.

Creating Happiness through a Balanced Luna

We balance our Luna by ensuring our thoughts, feelings, and perception of reality are objective, positive, and clear. This allows us to perceive ourselves and the world impartially without getting bogged down by misconceptions, fears, biases, and emotional upheavals. This frees our Luna energy—our imagination—to be expressed productively and creatively. When we balance our Luna, we radiate a positive energy that generates happiness both in us and in the people around us.

In a handprint, a balanced Luna will be roughly two-thirds the size of the Mount of Venus.

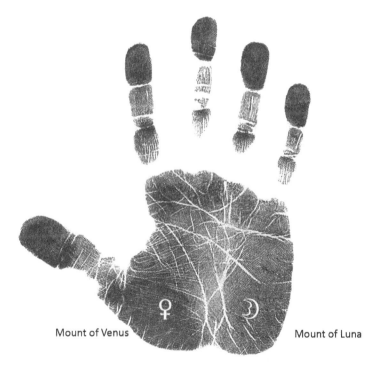

Mount of Venus   Mount of Luna

Fig. 3.7. A balanced Luna

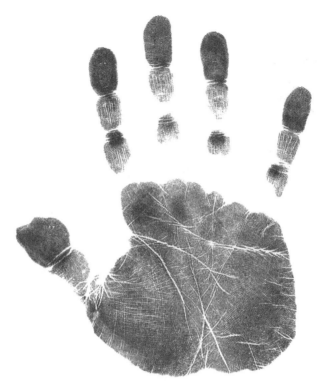

Fig. 3.8. An overactive Luna

The Overactive Luna

If our Luna is overactive, our sensory perception tends to be in overdrive. We crave excitement and stimulation, and if we don't find it, we will create drama in our lives. Often, our imagination will run wild, and we can become lost in our own imaginary world. We can easily lose our objectivity, becoming consumed with our personal desires and desensitized to the needs of those around us, creating an unhappy situation for all involved.

To restore balance to an overactive Luna, we must be more objective in our outlook and be more empathetic and sensitive to the needs of those around us. In short, we should make a conscious effort to balance our need for stimulation with an appropriate regard for others' happiness.

An overactive Luna will be roughly the same size or larger than the Mount of Venus.

The Underactive Luna

If our Luna is underactive, our imagination can turn against us, making us fearful, insecure, reticent, and restrained. Hence, with an undersized Luna, it is difficult to be free enough in ourselves to enjoy and appreciate all the world has to offer. We tend to see the proverbial glass half empty, which throws a wet blanket on our happiness.

The best way to restore balance to an underactive Luna is with a shift in attitude and outlook. In other words, we should start viewing the glass as half full, which we do by learning to appreciate all the good things in our lives, no matter how big or small—such as having a fresh cup of coffee in the morning, a nice apartment to come home to at the end of the day, or a few close friends or family members who care about us.

Keeping a daily gratitude journal can be very helpful in prompting our imagination to gradually envision the positive side of things rather than focusing on the negative.

An underactive Luna will be less than two-thirds the size of the Mount of Venus.

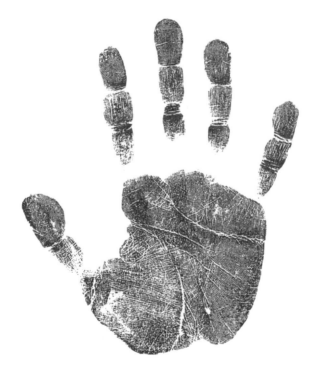

Fig. 3.9. An underactive Luna

The Mount of Venus

Our Body and the Appreciation of Love and Beauty

The Mount of Venus takes its name from the Roman goddess of love; it represents our physical body and the manner in which we experience and express love. As the largest mount in our hand, it is churning with the deepest forces of our nature: our survival instinct, our physical needs, longings, wants, and desires. It is the mount of beauty and is an expression of our appreciation and our love of life in all its forms, including nature, music, dancing, art, food and drink, romance, and all manner of entertainment.

But most importantly, Venus, as our body, is the temporary, flesh-and-blood home that our eternal soul inhabits during our earthly lifetime. In this sense, Venus is not only a reflection of our physicality, it is divinity incarnate and symbolic of all that is truly beautiful in life.

Creating Happiness through a Balanced Venus

We balance our Venus by not seeking our happiness solely through our own physical comfort and pleasure, but by taking joy in creating happiness for others. This can actually require us to travel out of our comfort zone to ensure the well-being of the people in our lives. Indeed, when we develop a balanced Venus, it brings out the sweetest qualities of our nature—our potential to love and be loveable; to be considerate and kind; and to bubble over with ananda, the joy of being alive.

A balanced Venus is generally one-third larger than the Mount of Luna.

The Overactive Venus

If our Venus is overactive, we tend to be driven by our survival instinct and our desire for comfort and pleasure. Constantly striving to satisfy our longings can lead to overindulgence, obsessive behavior, attachments, and even addictions. This attitude is obviously a recipe for disaster—it will rob us of happiness and could cause us to harm ourselves as well as everyone around us.

To correct an overactive Venus, we must learn to convert our longings and desires into devotion, selfless love, and some form of creativity. In other words, instead of obsessing over our personal gratification, we must incorporate a concern for the well-being and happiness of others in all we do.

It's hard to miss an overactive Venus because it tends to dominate the entire palm.

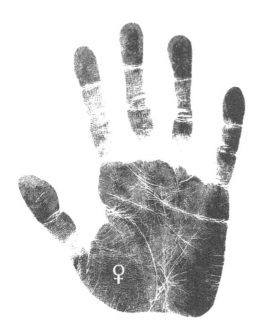

Fig. 3.10. A balanced Venus

Fig. 3.11. An overactive Venus

The Underactive Venus

When our Venus is underactive, we lack vitality and enthusiasm for life and can often feel listless, depleted, and indifferent. This will have a negative impact on our career, our relationships, our personal health and well-being, and, of course, the level of happiness we enjoy.

To restore balance to an underactive Venus, we must reengage with life and find a passion we can connect with. However, it is extremely difficult to start a fire without a spark, therefore we must ignite ourselves from within. To do this, we must begin with the physical by fueling our bodies with proper diet, getting an adequate amount of sleep, and exercising regularly. A healthy body will help regenerate us physically, mentally, and spiritually—thus allowing us to participate in the joy of living. Eventually, we will learn to appreciate what a true gift it is to be alive. Within a matter of months, we will likely notice that our Mount of Venus is beginning to fill out and that we are feeling much happier.

An underactive Mount of Venus can be equal to or less than the size of the Mount of Luna.

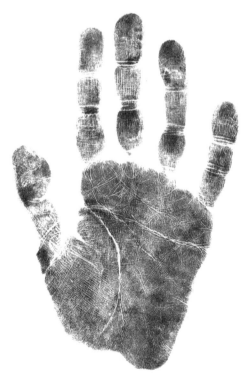

Fig. 3.12. An underactive Venus

The Mars Galaxy
OUR NOBLE WARRIOR SPIRIT

As mentioned earlier, the Mount of Mars is actually two mounts—Mars negative and Mars positive, known collectively as the Mars Galaxy. Mars negative is located above the Mount of Venus, and Mars positive is located on the other side of the palm, below the Mount of Mercury. In our tour around the palm, we have now reached Mars negative. But first we will take a moment to discuss the Mars Galaxy as a whole.

Mars negative relates to our physical energy, while Mars positive focuses on our mental attributes. A good analogy that illustrates the synergy between Mars negative and Mars positive is the long-distance runner. Running a successful marathon requires both physical energy and mental stamina. If we do not possess both physical strength (Mars negative) and willpower (Mars positive), we will not reach the finish line and complete the race.

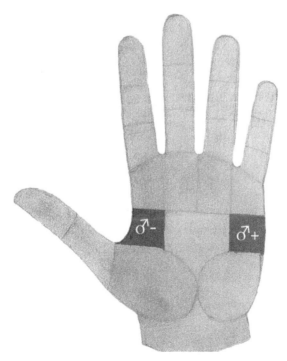

Fig. 3.13. Mars negative (♂-) and Mars positive (♂+)

THE BALANCED MARS GALAXY

In Roman mythology, the planet Mars represents the god of war. In the hand, a balanced Mars Galaxy represents the noble warrior. We are calm and composed in all situations while fearlessly facing the challenges of life; we champion worthy causes and stick up for the underdog.

In a handprint, both Mars negative and Mars positive have a smooth outer edge without any protrusion or indentation.

Mars Negative

Our Personal Force Field

As mentioned, Mars negative is the embodiment of our physical energy and strength. It drives us to get out of bed in the morning and get things done. It also allows us to defend ourselves and others if the need arises.

Mars negative also acts as our personal force field—it shields us from anything that threatens to distract our attention, disrupt our peace of mind, or cause us bodily harm.

Creating Happiness through a Balanced Mars Negative

To develop a balanced Mars negative, we must strive to be actively calm and calmly active. This enables us to live our life in a peaceful and productive manner; we do not waste our energy reacting to difficult situations or people by taking things personally and becoming defensive.

The Overactive Mars Negative

When our Mars negative is overactive, we are unable to control the way we respond to provocation—real or imagined. We are hotheaded, short-tempered, easily insulted, and quick to lash out with our tongue or our fists. An overactive Mars negative can lead to disastrous behavior that endangers our own health and safety and the well-being of those around us. When this is the case, our noble warrior becomes a bully and a thug.

Restoring balance to an overactive Mars negative requires us to release any pent-up Mars energy in a positive manner, such as fighting for the common good instead of fighting out of anger, disappointment, frustration, or rage.

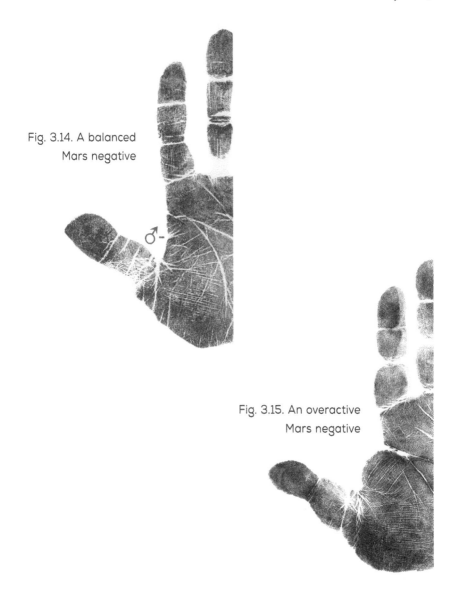

Fig. 3.14. A balanced
Mars negative

Fig. 3.15. An overactive
Mars negative

There is so much excess energy in an overactive Mars negative that it often reveals itself through a bulging protrusion on the edge of the mount.

The Underactive Mars Negative

When our Mars negative is underactive, we lack the stamina to tackle the challenges of life. Most of our Mars energy has been drained away;

we are like a warrior who has dropped his or her shield and is left unprotected and vulnerable on the battlefield. This will be expressed physically through a compromised immune system—we often feel stressed-out, worn down, and exhausted. Psychologically, we lack the wherewithal to defend our rights, champion a worthwhile cause, or fight for others; we too easily accept defeat and are quick to give up on our dreams. Like the marathon runner mentioned above, we need to develop the physical energy to reach the finish line.

The easiest and most effective way of restoring balance to an underactive Mars negative is by taking baby steps to reenergize our body and build up our stamina, such as assigning ourselves small daily tasks and goals that are not difficult to accomplish. By doing so, we will eventually build up our physical energy as well as develop self-confidence, endurance, fortitude, and initiative. In other words, our Mars warrior will once again possess the strength and nobility to pick up his or her shield, return to the battlefield, and resume fighting for the common good—our long distance runner will sail across the finish line.

The underactive Mars negative is so depleted of energy that it often reveals itself through an indentation on the edge of the mount.

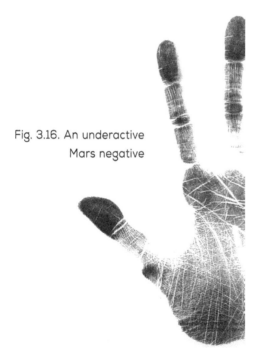

Fig. 3.16. An underactive
Mars negative

The Mount of Jupiter

Deciphering Our Life Purpose

The ancient seers of India referred to Jupiter as *Guru*, which translates as "dispeller of darkness." Jupiter pushes us to discover who we are as individuals, to seek out our own unique purpose in life, and to become the best human being we can be. In the process, Jupiter expands our horizons by developing a broader and more inclusive worldview.

Creating Happiness through a Balanced Jupiter

We balance our Mount of Jupiter by pursuing our ambition and seeking out our purpose in a calm, peaceful, and considerate fashion, ever careful not to disregard the rights or feelings of others. Indeed, we go out of our way to use our knowledge, gifts, and talents to help others and better the lives of those around us. Not surprisingly, Jupiter's predominate attributes are generosity, kindness, and magnanimity. Those blessed with a balanced Jupiter often become inspiring teachers, fair and just leaders, humanitarians, and philanthropists.

We know Jupiter is balanced when the length of the index finger reaches the halfway point of the distal phalange (tip) of the middle finger.

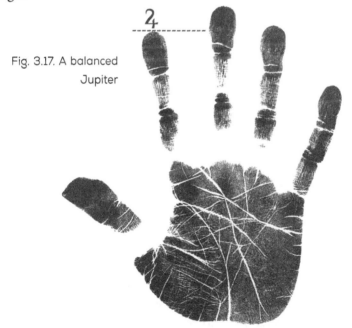

Fig. 3.17. A balanced Jupiter

The Overactive Jupiter

An overactive Jupiter reflects an overidentification with our ego, our public image, and the role we play in society. This sense of self-importance makes us susceptible to excessive pride, vanity, and arrogance. Our ego becomes a driving force in our life. We may become highly controlling in order to retain our status, attempting to dominate those around us. Indeed, we expect and rely on the praise, acknowledgment, and approval of others.

Restoring balance to an overactive Jupiter can be tricky because it requires a major shift in consciousness and attitude. We must come to see that our sense of self-worth must come from within and not be dependent on the recognition we receive from those around us, which can be fickle, false, and founded on fear instead of love and true admiration.

Hence, we must begin to identify with our heart rather than our ego. In doing so, we will balance our Jupiter energies by developing compassion, empathy, humility, and gratitude. In short (and to borrow a Yiddish word), we will become a *mensch*—a person of integrity and honor whom others will truly admire and respect.

We know Jupiter is overactive when the length of the index finger exceeds the halfway point of the distal phalange of the middle finger.

The Underactive Jupiter

When our Jupiter is underactive, we lack self-confidence and question our abilities. Although we may have ambition and a sense of purpose, we can easily lose our motivation and be overcome by a sense of futility, especially if we do not have a supportive environment. Consequently, the underactive Jupiter often suffers from low self-esteem. However, this does not mean we cannot accomplish a great deal. Often, in an effort to compensate for feelings of inadequacy, when we have an underactive Jupiter we will push ourselves to great heights and achieve incredible levels of success. But despite that success, we still have lingering doubts about our own self-worth, which can rob us of contentment, peace of mind, and happiness.

Restoring balance to an underactive Jupiter requires a change in outlook—we must convert doubt into belief. How? By ensuring we do everything we can to find and fulfill our purpose. We must place ourselves in a positive, supportive environment where we can more easily gain the skills and expertise we need to realize our goals. We will no longer focus on our perceived shortcomings—we will know that we are doing our best and have the talent, desire, and ability to achieve whatever it is we were put on this planet to accomplish. Our nagging self-doubts will be silenced and replaced with a sense of fulfillment and serenity, which are, of course, fundamental to happiness.

We know Jupiter is underactive when the length of the index finger doesn't reach the halfway point of the distal phalange of the middle finger.

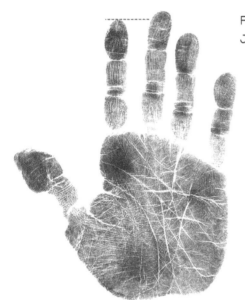

Fig. 3.18. An overactive Jupiter

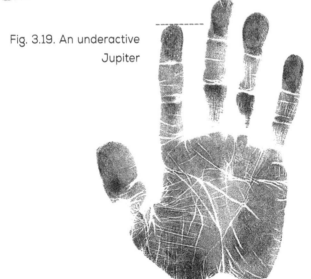

Fig. 3.19. An underactive Jupiter

The Mount of Saturn

A Potent Force for Change

Saturn is the mount of transformation. As fire transforms iron into steel, Saturn transforms the pain, hardship, and suffering we experience in life into awareness, wisdom, and compassion—it builds strength of character. Saturn teaches us to be introspective and contemplative, allowing us to seek out and discover the deepest truths about our real nature.

Creating Happiness through a Balanced Saturn

We balance our Saturn by letting go of past hurts and grievances—major happiness blockers. Rather than harboring those painful experiences, we must learn from them, which will make us wiser, more understanding, and compassionate. Furthermore, we must look at ourselves and our motivations honestly and objectively. This will provide us with a clarity of vision that cuts through falsehoods, illusion, and misconceptions, allowing us to discover the truth about ourselves and others. Through this we develop the integrity and moral fiber to assimilate, accept, and then express that truth in a fair, honest, and nonjudgmental manner. It is no surprise that those with a balanced Saturn are excellent mediators and judges. A balanced Saturn also supplies us with the discipline, focus, and structure to do what is needed to achieve our goals, fulfill our obligations, and pursue our purpose in life.

We know our Saturn is balanced when the length of the middle finger is equal to the width of the palm.

The Overactive Saturn

When our Saturn is overactive, we are not using its fiery energy to transform our pain and experiences in life into wisdom or personal growth. Instead, our penetrating vision tends to focus on the worst; we can be judgmental and overly critical of others. Consequently, it is hard for us to feel empathy or practice forgiveness. This isolates us from others, leaving us alone with our pessimistic thoughts.

The best way to restore balance to an overactive Saturn is by letting go of past hurts and resentments before we are consumed by them. To do this, we must direct the discipline and focus of Saturn toward helping others, which will increase our feelings of empathy and compas-

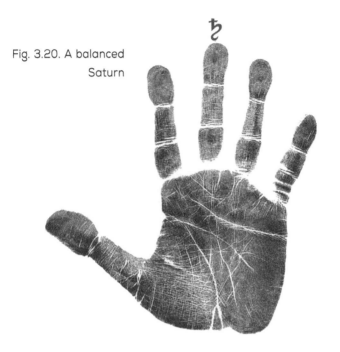

Fig. 3.20. A balanced Saturn

sion, as well as our ability to forgive. This will free us from the prison of our thoughts and allow us to happily rejoin the human race.

We know our Saturn is overactive when the length of the middle finger is longer than the width of the palm (see fig. 3.21 on page 52).

The Underactive Saturn

An underactive Saturn reflects poor judgment and an inability to envision the long-term consequences of our words and actions. We can be reckless in our behavior, negligent of our own health and safety, and insensitive to the needs and well-being of others.

The best way to restore balance to an underactive Saturn is by becoming more aware of our thoughts, words, and actions. For example, we could ask ourselves if it's appropriate to tell jokes at a funeral, or if it endangers others when we send a text message while we are driving. Bolstering Saturn's qualities of discipline, patience, and introspection will help us curb our impetuous nature. Meditation is an excellent tool that can help us in this regard.

We know our Saturn is underactive when the length of the middle finger is shorter than the width of the palm (see fig. 3.22 on page 52).

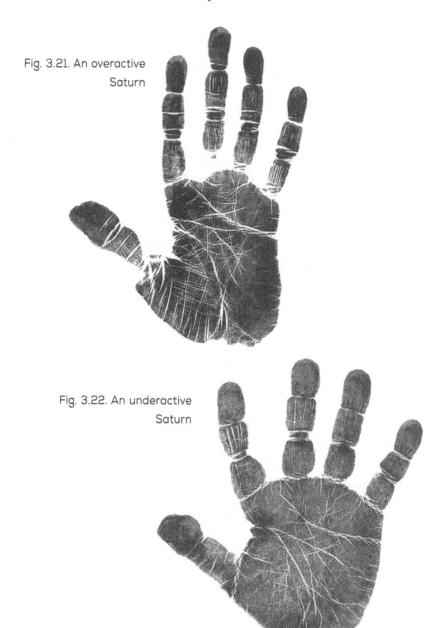

Fig. 3.21. An overactive
Saturn

Fig. 3.22. An underactive
Saturn

The Mount of Sun

Attracting Your Heart's Desires

The Mount of Sun directly connects us to our heart and feelings of
universal love. Just as the physical Sun is a radiating body of unimagi-

nable light and heat, the force of our personal Sun radiates a strength and magnetism like no other mount. And because the Mount of Sun is the mount most closely associated with our heart and soul, tapping into our Sun energy plugs us into the universal life force. This accounts for the passion, conviction, and self-assuredness with which we pursue our purpose in life, as well as the optimism and highly charged charisma we radiate once we have awakened our Sun energy.

Creating Happiness through a Balanced Sun

We develop a balanced Sun by striving to be our most authentic self. We have no secret agenda and freely share the best of ourselves with others without hesitation or expectation. Developing our Sun energy allows us to vibrate with loving feelings and exude a genuine sense of happiness and joy that others find irresistible. To enjoy the best qualities our Sun has to offer, we need to tap into the depths of our heart and dedicate ourselves to our true passion. This will allow our natural gifts and talents to shine brilliantly and inspire others. But the real beauty of Sun is that, no matter how popular we become or how much

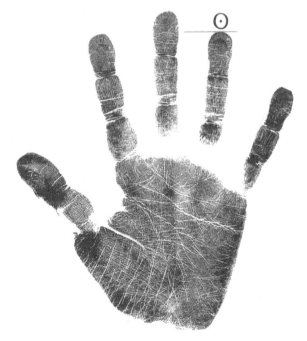

Fig. 3.23. A balanced Sun

success and fame we enjoy, we always remain humble with a heart that is ever open and loving.

We know Sun is balanced when the length of the ring finger reaches the halfway point of the distal phalange of the middle finger.

The Overactive Sun

When our Sun is overactive, we place enormous expectations on those around us to live up to our own high standards. When people fail to meet our expectations, misunderstandings, disappointment, and heartache often ensue. Indeed, our heart may shut down, leaving us angry, disillusioned, and despondent. It has often been said that no one falls harder than a wounded Sun.

The best way to restore balance to an overactive Sun is by managing our expectations. We can achieve this by remaining humble and conscientious, which helps ensure that we always express our love and affection for others with no strings attached. In other words, we do our utmost to practice unconditional love.

We know Sun is overactive when the length of the ring finger exceeds the halfway point of the distal phalange of the middle finger.

The Underactive Sun

When the Sun is underactive, our radiant Sun energy is hidden behind a cloud. Our mind is absorbed in self-doubt and insecurity, which makes it difficult for us to connect with our heart. Hence, we do not exude the confidence and self-assurance associated with a balanced Mount of Sun.

To restore balance to an underactive Sun, we must reconnect with our heart. How? By recognizing the divine spark that exists within us all. This recognition will allow us to offer up our self-doubts and insecurities to our own higher power. We can achieve this through regular meditation, prayer, and/or by being of service to others. Soon, the cloud blocking our Sun energy will disappear; we will not only feel good about ourselves but will not feel threatened by the happiness and success of others.

We know Sun is underactive when the length of the ring finger doesn't reach the halfway point of the distal phalange of the middle finger.

Fig. 3.24. An
overactive Sun

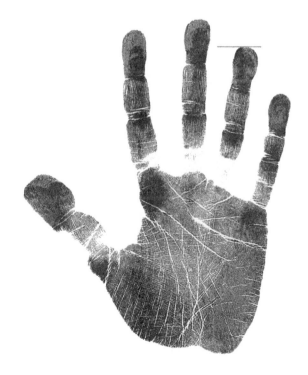

Fig. 3.25. An
underactive Sun

The Mount of Mercury

The Art of Self-Expression

Mercury is all about communication. It is no coincidence that the Mount of Mercury takes its name from the wing-footed messenger god of Roman mythology—Mercury—who sped through the Cosmos delivering divinely inspired messages to the gods and mortals alike. Mercury not only allows us to express our thoughts and ideas clearly and eloquently, but it also gives us the ability to pick up on nonverbal clues; we empathetically understand the body language, moods, and needs of those around us. Furthermore, Mercury can directly connect us with the Cosmos—it gives us the power to intuitively plug into the Akash, which, according to Eastern texts, is an ethereal record of the wisdom of the ages. Indeed, many of the inspired ideas of artists, philosophers, and scientists that have changed the world for the better have come to them through their Mercury-Akash connection.

Creating Happiness through a Balanced Mercury

Mercury is the mount of detachment and helps us put our problems into perspective. It teaches us to laugh at our own follies, find the humor in the human condition, and smile in the face of adversity. This is why Mercury is known as the mount of transcendence—its ethereal nature allows us to detach from expectations and lifts us above our personal hurts to a state of joy.

Indeed, when we experience even a moment of that joy, we are freed from the grip pain and disappointment have on us. We thus detach from the expectations we have placed on others, making room in our heart for empathy to take root and flourish.

We can balance our Mercury by learning to live in the moment happily absorbed in whatever work or task with which we are occupied. Consequently, hours will fly by like minutes as we are contented with who we are and what we are doing. Because we are not focused on the fruits of our actions, we are not burdened by expectation and attachments. Hence, we express ourselves freely and enjoy life, which we embrace with gratitude, a sense of humor, and a smile on our face. We create, perform, and communicate our ideas and talents for the sheer joy of self-expression. We can further balance our Mercury by develop-

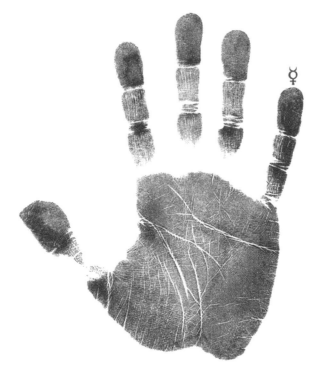

Fig. 3.26. A balanced Mercury

ing our ability to heal, which we do by attuning to the needs of others, being good listeners, and offering words of advice.

We know Mercury is balanced when the length of the little finger reaches the distal phalange of the ring finger.

The Overactive Mercury

When our Mercury energy is overactive, we become overly attached to the fruits of our actions and the pleasures of the material world. We lose the capacity to enjoy living in the moment because we are occupied with what we can get and possess. We may become so focused on what we want—be it money, sex, or a Nobel Prize—that we lose our moral compass, disregard our conscience, and abandon our powers of discernment. Our attachment to the external material world inevitably comes at the expense of our happiness and inner harmony.

To restore balance to an overactive Mercury, we must learn to communicate honestly and from the heart rather than in a self-serving manner. To do this, we must develop a Buddha-like approach to life and living in which we value peace of mind and spiritual growth over material gain, fame, and physical pleasure. A strong Mercury provides us with the skills and talent to play a major role on the world stage. But with this power comes great responsibility—we must use our gifts for the good of humankind, and not personal profit. In doing so, we will find happiness and pleasure in each moment; we will enjoy the journey of life and not be solely obsessed with the destination.

We know Mercury is overactive when the length of the little finger extends beyond the distal phalange of the ring finger.

The Underactive Mercury

When our Mercury energy is underactive, we don't possess the where-withal to express ourselves freely. Indeed, we have little interest in communicating with the world around us; we lack curiosity about current events or what is happening beyond our front door. Indeed, we value our tranquility so much we often isolate ourselves to avoid excitement, disruption, or conflict.

To restore balance to an underactive Mercury, we must find ways of maintaining our sense of peace and tranquility without retreating from the world due to nervousness, fear, anxiety, or a reluctance to express ourselves in public. To achieve this, we should seek fun and enjoyable avenues of creative self-expression, such as taking an art class, dancing, or joining a public-speaking group. Having faced our fears, we will be able to establish happiness and peace of mind without having to hide from the world.

We know Mercury is underactive when the length of the little finger doesn't reach the distal phalange of the ring finger.

Mars Positive

Mental Endurance and Moral Fortitude

As we've learned, Mars positive represents our mental energy. It is associated with our executive brain, which is responsible for reasoning, problem-solving, and decision-making. It fuels the passion needed to materialize our present and future dreams, as well as to complete any unfinished tasks we have carried with us from the past.

Mars positive provides us with the strength of mind needed to

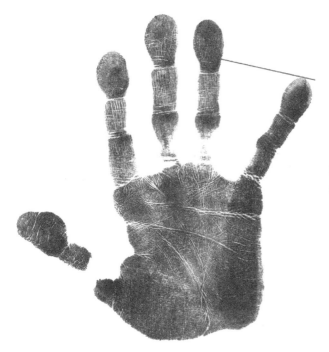

Fig. 3.27. An
overactive Mercury

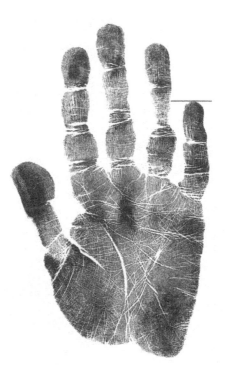

Fig. 3.28. An
underactive Mercury

control and direct our physical (Mars negative) energy in a positive and productive direction.

Creating Happiness through a Balanced Mars Positive

To develop a balanced Mars positive, we must maintain our self-composure in all circumstances. With this level-headed approach to life, we remain objective, charged with a laser-sharp mental focus through which we can make good choices, problem-solve, and overcome obstacles blocking us from happiness. Even though a balanced Mars positive gives us intense drive and passion, our thoughts and actions remain calm and peaceful. Creating a balanced Mars positive requires us to practice patience, build endurance, exercise willpower, and develop concentration. This will give us nerves of steel that shield us from fear, worry, and anxiety.

In a handprint, a balanced Mars positive has a smooth outer edge without any protrusion or indentation.

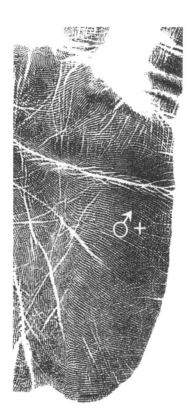

Fig. 3.29. A balanced Mars positive

The Overactive Mars Positive

When our Mars positive is overactive, our mental energy has gone into hyperdrive. There is so much excess energy in Mars positive that we are fueled by an unbridled zeal to get what we want; hence, we no longer pursue our goals peaceably or with detachment. We can be possessive and willing to override the needs and rights of others to lay claim to what we feel is rightfully ours.

To restore balance to an overactive Mars positive, we must let go of our sense of ownership. When we try to control and possess material things and people, we end up prisoners of our own attachments and desires—and in that prison there is no happiness. Instead of using our enormous Mars energy trying to force people to love us or do what we want, we can make a huge difference in the world—and our own happiness—by channeling that energy into a noble and worthy cause.

An overactive Mars positive protrudes outward from the side of the hand.

Fig. 3.30. An overactive Mars positive

The Underactive Mars Positive

When our Mars positive is underactive, we lack the mental stamina to simply complete day-to-day tasks. We do not feel empowered in our daily life and interactions with others. Indeed, we can give up too easily when faced with a difficult problem or challenge. Because we can't rely on ourselves, we become dependent in our relationships with others for support and inspiration.

Restoring balance to an underactive Mars positive requires us to develop greater strength and fortitude—we must become self-reliant. We must find a cause to fight for or a mission that gives our life purpose. Having a sense of what to live and breathe for will rekindle our passion, ignite our Mars energy, and help us recognize that life is a great gift. This passion, purpose, and appreciation of life will quickly awaken our Mars warrior.

An underactive Mars positive will be indented on the side of the hand.

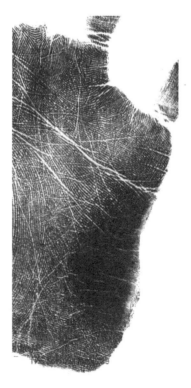

Fig. 3.31. An underactive Mars positive

Rahu and Ketu
UNDERSTANDING YOUR KARMIC MISSION

As we've learned, the mounts of Rahu and Ketu are all about our karma; these two mounts are inextricably intertwined. Ketu represents the circumstances we attracted in the past and embodies our attitudes and reactions to those circumstances. Rahu represents our current circumstances and immediate environment. A famous Sanskrit verse tells us that "our present is the result of all our yesterdays and our future depends on how well we live today." This sums up the relationship between Rahu and Ketu. The big question is . . . are we willing, ready, and able to make the most of our present circumstances? Or will we resist the opportunities that come our way and become prisoners of our past, which will inevitably jeopardize both our happiness and our future?

This is why, when it comes to creating happiness, we must study both mounts. Let's begin with Ketu.

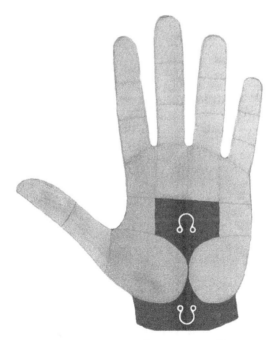

Fig. 3.32. Rahu (☊) and Ketu (☋)

The Mount of Ketu

Our Window to the Past

Ketu tells us how much karma we are bringing with us from our past lifetime to our present lifetime, and how well we are dealing with that karma—both of which will determine the strength of our first tentative steps into our new life's journey. Consequently, the quality of this mount indicates how our future, and future happiness, may unfold.

Creating Happiness through a Balanced Ketu

To bring out the best of our Ketu, we must approach life with a "live and let live" attitude. We need to fearlessly embrace the journey of our current lifetime; we are neither intimidated by others nor seek to interfere with the journey they are on. We strive to use the wisdom acquired in the past to deal with our new karma calmly and objectively.

Ketu is balanced when the width of the wrist is equal to the collective width of the mounts of Jupiter, Saturn, and Sun.

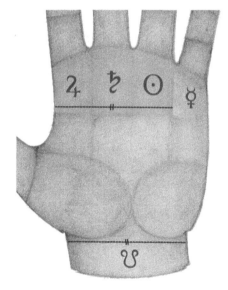

Fig. 3.33. A balanced Ketu

The Overactive Ketu

An overactive Ketu indicates that we have entered this lifetime with a bag full of unfulfilled desires; we are overly eager to rush headlong into

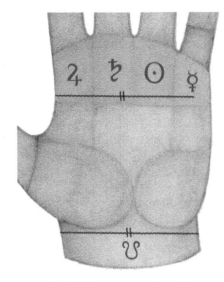

Fig. 3.34. An overactive Ketu

new experiences without taking the time to digest and benefit from our past karmic lessons. As a result, we may build up more negative karma, which we will have to deal with in this life or the next. As Russell Crowe's character, Maximus, says in the movie *Gladiator*: "What we do in this life echoes through eternity."

To restore balance to an overactive Mount of Ketu, we must develop a proper sense of judgment—one that is tempered with discernment and reflection—before embarking on any new venture.

Ketu is overactive when the width of the wrist exceeds the collective width of the mounts of Jupiter, Saturn, and Sun and extends into the Mount of Mercury.

The Underactive Ketu

An underactive Ketu suggests that we entered our current lifetime very tentatively due to unresolved inhibitions, fears, and anxieties. We tend not to stray far from the people, places, and things that provide us with comfort and security. Instead of being self-reliant, we look to others to support, inspire, and motivate us.

To restore balance to an underactive Mount of Ketu, we must find the courage to move forward in life and find an environment in which we can develop our talents and find a purpose in life. Facing our fears

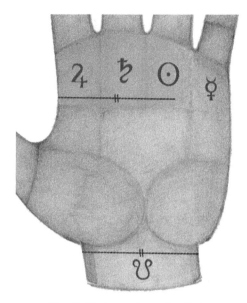

Fig. 3.35. An underactive Ketu

is the first step in resolving the karmic issues that have been holding us back—and a giant leap toward happiness.

Ketu is underactive when the width of the wrist is less than the collective width of the mounts of Jupiter, Saturn, and Sun.

The Mount of Rahu

The Past Made Present

Rahu represents our present environment and how willingly we embark on new experiences and act on new opportunities. For example, do we embrace opportunities that come our way with gratitude and appreciation, or do we let them slip away? The energy of Rahu allows us to make the most of our present circumstances and find happiness in the moment.

Creating Happiness through a Balanced Rahu

We develop a balanced Rahu by being grateful for the people in our lives and freely embracing the opportunities that come our way. By learning from our past-life lessons, we develop the wisdom and discernment needed to approach the future with a clear and optimistic vision. When Rahu is balanced, we are happy and in harmony with

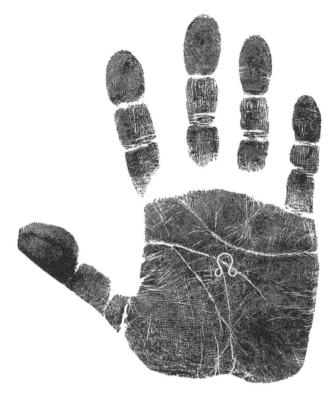

Fig. 3.36. A balanced Rahu

our surroundings; our immediate environment is fully supporting us on our life's journey.

In the hand, a balanced Rahu appears as a gentle valley in the center of the palm surrounded by the other mounts.

The Overactive Rahu

An overactive Rahu suggests that we are so fixated on getting what we want in the present that we can undermine our future possibilities. For example, instead of appreciating being entrusted to manage the finances of a charity, we choose to embezzle the funds to pay for a lavish vacation. However, when our activities are discovered, we will not only lose our job, our standing in the community, and the respect of our family and friends, we may end up with a criminal record that curtails our future prospects. Even worse, our actions have caused pain and suffering to those we most love, creating a boatload of karma for ourselves.

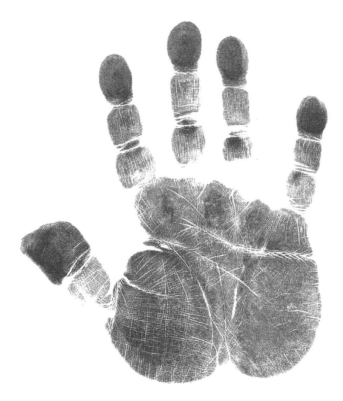

Fig. 3.37. An overactive Rahu

To bring balance to an overactive Rahu, we must develop enough wisdom, discernment, and awareness to appreciate the consequences of our actions. Consequently, we also need to develop long-term vision, recognizing that our immediate environment is merely one step on a much longer spiritual journey. Perhaps the most effective way to achieve this is by connecting with our higher self through meditation, which will help us to reflect on our actions, become more discerning, and develop a greater sense of empathy and compassion.

In the hand, an overactive Rahu will be flush with the surrounding mounts.

The Underactive Rahu

When our Rahu is underactive, we feel disconnected from our current environment and may consequently miss out on opportunities. We tend to be easily overwhelmed by the circumstances that surround us.

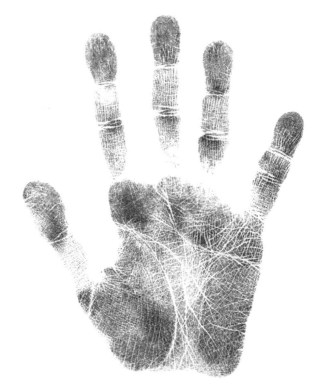

Fig. 3.38. An underactive Rahu

To restore balance to an underactive Rahu, we need to reach out to those who understand our situation and are willing to support and motivate us. With enough dedication and encouragement, we will be able to realize our full potential, make the most of the opportunities presented to us, and create a happy life.

An underactive Rahu appears as a steep ditch in the center of the palm.

◆◆◆

Achieving happiness through palmistry means we have to first achieve balance in all the mounts we have just discussed. However, three of those mounts are particularly important to master in order to ensure a fully happy life—the triad of Luna-Venus-Mars negative, which we will tackle in our next chapter.

Tripling Our Chances for Happiness

The Luna-Venus-Mars Triad

More than 2,500 years ago the Greek poet Hesiod wrote: "A bad neighbor is a misfortune, as much as a good one is a great blessing." Those words have rung true throughout the ages.

Having well-balanced neighbors who are courteous, caring, and supportive helps us to live happier and more peaceful lives. On the other

Fig. 4.1. Good neighbors are a great blessing.

hand, neighbors who yell and scream all day and blast their music all night long can quickly destroy our equilibrium, rob of us of our sleep, undermine our peace of mind, and basically make our life miserable.

The same principle applies to the mounts, especially when it comes to Venus and its neighboring mounts of Mars negative and Luna. Why? Because for Venus to express its natural qualities of love and joy, it must rely on the healthy perceptions of Luna and the peaceful energy of the action-oriented Mars negative. As Venus is sandwiched between these two powerhouse mounts, any imbalances in Luna or Mars can put the brakes on our ability to love and be happy. Let's find out more about the Luna-Venus-Mars triad.

UNDERSTANDING THE TRIAD OF HAPPINESS

Luna (☽) is the storehouse of our sensory (incoming) nerves, and Mars (♂) is the storehouse of our motor (outgoing) nerves. In other words, the Mount of Luna determines how we perceive the world, and Mars determines how we react to those perceptions. But neither our perceptions nor our reactions could be expressed in the real world without the cooperation of Venus (♀). Why? Well, as we have learned, Venus represents our physical body and is therefore home to our sensory and motor organs—our eyes, ears, mouth, feet, hands, and so forth. Consequently, our perceptions, related to Luna, and our reactions to those perceptions, fueled by the energy of Mars, can only be physically expressed through Venus. When Luna and Mars negative are balanced, our expression of Venus will be based on kindness, consideration, and love.

However, an imbalanced Mount of Luna can easily misinterpret situations and, when combined with the potentially volatile nature of Mars energy, we may end up disturbing the health, peace, and loving nature of our Mount of Venus. When the perceptions of Luna ignite a negative Mars reaction, our body (Venus) enters the fight-or-flight mode, which disrupts all of Venus's wonderful qualities in multiple ways. Indeed, it can hinder our ability to give and receive love, undermine the harmony of our relationships, and decrease our ability to enjoy the simple pleasures and natural beauty that Venus allows us to appreciate—like a child's laughter, a beautiful sunset, sharing a delicious meal with friends

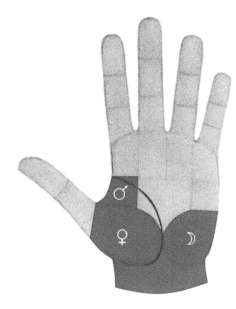

Fig. 4.2. The triad of Luna (☽) – Venus (♀) – Mars (♂)

and family, or listening to a Mozart symphony . . . the things that add sweetness to our existence and can make life truly enjoyable.

Consequently, imbalances in Luna and Mars can make us act in ways that are contrary to Venus's nurturing impulses. For example, instead of helping or healing others with our hands, we may hit or punch them; instead of using our words to be kind and consoling, we may be sarcastic and cruel; and instead of gravitating toward positive situations that will bring us success and happiness, we could be drawn to environments that are unhealthy or dangerous for us. Indeed, given Luna's potential for misinterpreting sensory information, and Mars's potentially malefic and warlike nature, the loving aspects of Venus are vulnerable to attack when either of its neighbors are imbalanced. And when that happens we can easily create negative karma—and a lot of unnecessary unhappiness.

On the other hand, a balanced Mars negative and a balanced Luna will be excellent neighbors and help Venus express its most loving qualities, filling our lives with happiness and joy.

Let's take a look at how these scenarios can play out in our daily life by examining the handprints of some Birla Center clients. We will start with Lise, who enjoys a great deal of harmony in her mounts of Luna, Venus, and Mars negative.

LISE'S STORY
A Balanced Triad:
A Nurturing Heart and a Passion for Beauty

As we see in her handprint, Lise's mounts of Luna, Venus, and Mars negative are all well-shaped; in other words, they are neither protruding (overactive) nor flaccid and indented (underactive). This, as we learned in our last chapter, tells us that these mounts are balanced, which means her Luna-Venus-Mars triad is in a state of harmony.

That harmony provided Lise with a healthy and vibrant imagination, creative energy, and an unrelenting passion to turn her love of beauty into a multimillion-dollar cosmetics empire. Venus's love of family inspired her to include her husband and daughters in the business, which made the enterprise both joyous and profitable. Even more inspiring, the harmony within her triad prompted her to create a philanthropic foundation that has helped hundreds of women reach their full potential.

LISE

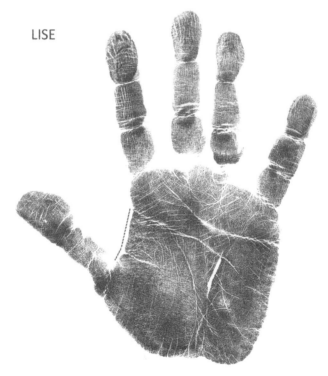

Fig. 4.3. A balanced Luna-Venus-Mars triad

Lise's life can serve as an inspiration for us all; by mastering the energies of our triad, we will not only bring happiness to ourselves but to all the people in our lives.

✦✦✦

BENOIT'S STORY

An Imbalanced Triad: Insecurity and Rage

Benoit has an imbalanced triad; his Mount of Venus is squeezed between a shrunken, underactive Luna (its base is missing) and an overactive Mars negative. We know Mars is overactive because there is a bulge protruding from it, a negative feature we'll discuss in greater detail a little later in this chapter. Unfortunately, the misperceptions of Benoit's faulty Luna convinced him that his girlfriend was being unfaithful, triggering his hyperactive Mars to act out aggressively. Indeed, in a fit of jealous rage, Benoit physically attacked the woman he professed to love and ended up serving time for his crime.

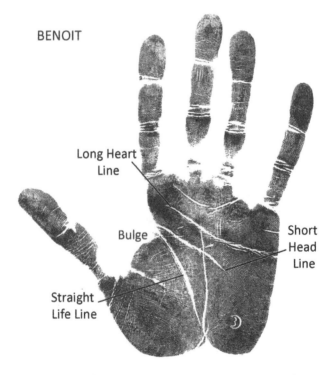

Fig. 4.4. An imbalanced Luna-Venus-Mars triad

We'll begin studying the major lines in our next chapters; for now, suffice it to say that Benoit's long Heart Line shows he is idealistic, but his long, straight Life Line (which should, ideally, gently curve around the Venus mount) undermines the loving nature of Venus, making him extremely demanding and inflexible.

Furthermore, his short Head Line creates an imbalanced *quadrangle*, the space between the Heart and Head lines, which, when well-formed, draws supportive friends and positive circumstances into our lives. All of this denotes a shortsightedness that prevented him from envisioning the long-term consequences of his actions. Rather than roll with the punches and go with the flow, Benoit was rigidly determined to follow his own path, a path that led to tragedy and prison.

LUNA

Doorway to Healing or Illness

Over the past several decades a copious amount of research has illustrated the strong connection between body and mind, and that our thinking directly impacts our mental, emotional, physical, and spiritual health. That is why, in our quest to be happy, we need to understand and master the Mount of Luna—the mount of perception where all of our thoughts and feelings are generated.

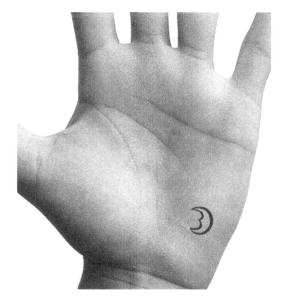

Fig. 4.5. The Mount of Luna: Doorway to healing or illness

Indeed, science is proving that our thoughts can actually produce physiological changes in the body. For example, we may step on a piece of rope but mistakenly *think* it is a snake, and our imagination runs wild. Even though we are in no real danger, we *think* we are, and those thoughts trigger our fight-or-flight response, resulting in a sudden release of adrenalin, a pounding heart, and a panicked state of mind where all we can focus on is either killing the snake or running away from it. There is no room for happiness when in fight-or-flight mode. Indeed, finding happiness is difficult when even mundane troubles begin shading our thoughts, like being late for work or getting to the grocery store before it closes.

Hence, in order to be happy, we must be conscious of our thoughts and always remember that we can feel better and be happier by changing the way we think. A simple example of this is using our imagination and power of our visualization to see the proverbial glass as being half full instead of half empty. In short, the Mount of Luna can be a doorway to happiness and healing or a fast track to anxiety and illness. It all depends on how we decide to think and choose to perceive things, a basic truth echoed by the modern-day Hindu guru Amma.

Widely known as the "hugging saint," Amma has filled venues around the globe and is said to have hugged more than 36 million people worldwide. When asked by a *New York Daily News* reporter about the connection between thinking and happiness, she responded: "One person looks at a flower, he will think about the joyous moments he spent with his beloved. But when another person looks at that same flower, he remembers how his lover jilted him. But the flower remains the flower. Both of these emotions are created by the mind. Just like any other decision, happiness is also a decision."

Hence, we must actively choose to be happy, which we can do by gaining mastery over the source of our thoughts, feelings, and imagination—the Mount of Luna. If our Luna is imbalanced, our thoughts will be too. A balanced Luna provides us with the guidance of objective perception, without which we can fall victim to the happiness blockers of subjectivity and misperception.

Now let's take a look at the second mount of the triad: Venus, the mount of love; and love, of course, is essential in our quest for happiness.

Fig. 4.6. Amma, the "hugging saint"

VENUS

The Biggest Kid on the Block

To experience love, we need to tap into the finest and most balanced qualities of Venus—care, kindness, compassion, and empathy. However, that can be tricky as Venus is the largest mount in the hand and churns with the energy of deep-seated desires and urges. Venus relates to our body and all the issues that come with it: our physical survival, security, comfort, and a deep primal instinct to seek pleasure and avoid pain. Indeed, we are up against a lot when striving for balance in Venus.

We can be driven by powerful longings and desires that can lead to painful attachments. We can become bound to anything that promises us pleasure or relief from emotional pain and the stresses of life, such as cigarettes, coffee, food, sex, drugs, or alcohol. Our attachments can also extend beyond material things and lock us into emotional mindsets that convince us we will only be happy when our desires are satisfied, such as being in a relationship, earning straight A's at school, and beating out the competition to get the job or promotion we want. And while

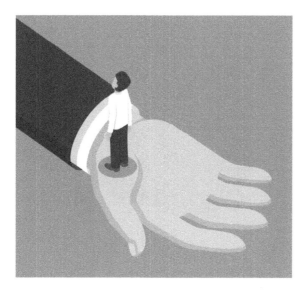

Fig. 4.7. Venus, the largest mount in the hand—home of human needs, longings, and desires

those things may give us momentary satisfaction, they will not bring us lasting happiness. In the end, our attachments weigh us down and make us miserable. To be truly happy we need balance in Venus, and the quickest way to bring our Venus back to balance is by letting go of our attachments.

Stop Monkeying Around

Let Go of Attachments

Ram Dass, the American spiritual teacher, psychologist, and author, once shared a story about dealing with our attachments by describing how they catch wild monkeys in India. He told his audience that the monkey catcher drops a handful of nuts into a jar with a small opening. The monkey puts his hand into the jar, grabs the nuts, and then finds that he can't get his fist out through the opening. If the monkey would just let go of the nuts, he could escape. But he won't. Attachment leads to suffering, Ram Dass concluded. It's as simple as that: Letting go of attachments leads to freedom.

But what happens when our attachments are so visceral that to let go of them feels like letting go of life itself?

To bring our Venus back to balance we have to practice detachment. Unlike the monkey, we know that to regain our freedom we have to let go of the nuts. However, this is not easy to do. When we're dealing with

Fig. 4.8. Letting go of attachments

strong attachments, we need to begin by acknowledging and working with our feelings. We have to ask ourselves what is driving us to such an extent that we are losing our peace and getting caught in the cycle of the excited desire we feel when we want something, the anxiety we feel about losing it, and the sense of hopelessness that can arise when we fail to achieve it and we have to face the loss.

So, we have to ask, when we can feel the joy of life, why choose to suffocate ourselves in longings, desires, and obsessions? As the largest mount, Venus is overflowing with powerful, primal energy, which we never want to lose because it fuels our passion and is the essence of life. Fortunately, with some recalibration, and a little effort and discipline, we can channel that abundant energy into altruistic and spiritual directions that will enrich our lives and better the world.

Here are four practical techniques that can help you recalibrate your Venus energy and deal with attachments that can lead to negative habits or unproductive ways of thinking that block our happiness. In other words, they are tips for a happier life.

✳ Alternate Nostril Breathing

According to the late great Vedic scholar, poet, and musician Harish Johari in *Breath, Mind, and Consciousness*, we can break bad habits and transform negative moods into positive ones by utilizing a simple technique known as alternate nostril breathing.

Fig. 4.9. Alternate nostril breathing

Harish explains that breath coming in through the right nostril cools the right hemisphere of the brain, causing the left hemisphere to become active, and vice versa. Hence, alternating the nostril through which we breathe creates a shift in our perception. Consequently, we can immediately change our mindset by taking a moment to check which nostril we are inhaling from. Simply by closing that nostril with a finger, we force the breath to be inhaled and exhaled through the opposite nostril, instantaneously creating a new and more positive way of viewing the world and dealing with our problems. (More detailed instructions are provided in the Happiness Booster beginning on the bottom of page 142.)

✳ Emotional Freedom Technique (EFT)

EFT, now commonly referred to as "tapping," is similar to acupuncture as it focuses on the body's meridian points (energy centers) to restore balance. While acupuncture uses needles to apply pressure to the meridian points, EFT applies pressure with finger tapping.

Tapping on these centers in the sequence listed below sends signals to the part of the brain that controls stress, helping to relieve the painful symptoms caused by negative experiences or emotions and the effects of trauma. While keeping in mind whatever is troubling you, use your fingertips to tap five to seven times on the following meridian points:

Fig. 4.10. Tapping:
Emotional Freedom Technique

- ♦ Eyebrows
- ♦ Both sides of the eyes
- ♦ Under the eyes
- ♦ Chin
- ♦ Collarbones
- ♦ Underarms
- ♦ Top of the head

In his book *The Tapping Solution*, Nick Ortner calls EFT a powerful way "to interrupt, disengage, dissolve, and vanquish negative patterns. Tapping gets to the root of what's going on, balancing the mind and body, and changing what we do, how we feel, and how we experience the world."

It's through that balance that we establish harmony in Venus.

✳ Self-Reflection and Meditation

The most powerful way to recalibrate our Venus energy is through self-reflection and meditation, which allows us to tap into the hidden reservoir of bliss within us. The deeper our awareness, the more we will realize Venus is the temporary physical home of our infinite soul, which exists in a state of perfect bliss. By looking deep within our own

Fig. 4.11. Recalibrating our Venus energy through
self-reflection and meditation

nature, we can experience a joy that is not dependent on any outward event, person, or thing. As Paramahansa Yogananda says in *The Divine Romance*: "When you sit in the silence of deep meditation, joy bubbles up from within, roused by no outer stimulus. The joy of meditation is overwhelming."

✳ *Accessing the Power of Universal Love*

Perhaps the attachment most difficult for us to shed is our habit of seeing others as being separate from ourselves. This is a perfectly normal way of seeing things, at least from the purely physical viewpoint of Venus. After all, in the material world, our flesh-and-blood body does make us self-contained and separate from others. Unfortunately, that perspective is a happiness blocker.

When we see others, we see their body and personality; we don't see their true self, their soul, through which all of us are linked. So, if we want to "love our neighbor as we love ourself," we must discover our true self and learn to love it!

Once we do that, our Venus can shift from being the mount of

Fig. 4.12. We are all connected through Spirit.

our personal identity and survival instinct to our mount of nurturing, caring love. This is when we recognize the soul in every person and realize that we are all connected through Spirit—a connection that is guaranteed to bring us happiness.

When we fully resonate with the best of our Venus energy, the sweetest qualities of our nature will rise to the surface of our being and radiate to others—we will love and be lovable, be considerate and kind, exude innocence and enthusiasm, and bubble over with the joy of being alive.

Now that we have a better understanding of Venus, let's turn our attention to the third mount of the triad—Mars negative, reflecting our inner warrior, which can either bring out the joy of Venus or create unhappiness and disruption in our lives and the lives of those around us. Indeed, mastering our Mars energy is an essential step in our quest for happiness.

MARS NEGATIVE

Beauty and the Beast

If people are able to push our emotional buttons and make us temporarily lose our mind and respond unreasonably, which we can later

Fig. 4.13. Mars negative: Beauty and the Beast

regret, there is a strong likelihood our Mars energy is imbalanced and in need of a tune-up. If people's negative comments or miserable attitudes mess up our day, it's further evidence Mars is in need of fortification. Indeed, if we have no control over our reactive nature, no matter how small the perceived insult, it is a sign we need to master our Mars inner warrior.

Through Mars, all things are possible—it is the nuclear power plant of the palm and, when mastered, will carry us through a joyful and happy life. But when neglected or misused, it can wreak havoc upon us.

Throughout history, Mars has always been regarded as the god of war. So it isn't surprising that our Mars negative possesses a warrior energy. Indeed, one of the most important things we can do in palmistry is train our inner warrior to be peaceful and noble, not belligerent, aggressive, or thoughtless. Proper training is what makes the difference between Mars being a positive or negative force in our life.

Mars enables us to maintain our cool no matter what life throws at us or how unfairly others treat us. When mastered, Mars will provide us with the mental and emotional strength and composure to face difficulties and adversity with true courage. But when neglected or misused, our Mars energy can create a perfect storm of erratic impulses, emotional volatility, aggression, and rage that can destroy our happiness. In short, an excessive, out-of-control Mars can turn even a noble warrior into a beast.

However, if we can control our Mars, we will be virtually impervious to the slings and arrows of life. Like insulation on an electrical wire, it will shield us from harmful shocks and stresses to our nerves and immune system. But, with an uncontrolled Mars, we will be wounded by every arrow and outrage life hurls our way or strike out at anyone who crosses us.

Mars and Venus
A SPECIAL RELATIONSHIP

It is Mars negative's job to protect his lovely next-door neighbor, Venus, the mount of beauty, love, and sweetness. Protecting

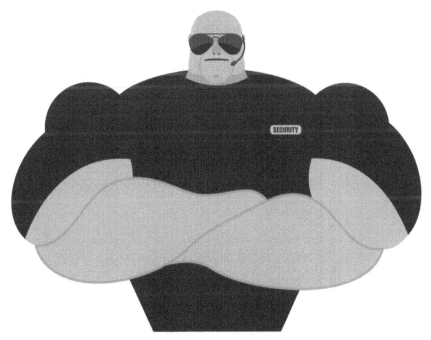

Fig. 4.14. Mars negative is Venus's personal bodyguard.

Venus from stress and aggression enables us to remain true to our loving, nurturing nature. Fortunately, as our inner warrior, Mars negative understands aggression and knows how to deal with it in a self-composed manner; it is able to deflect and turn away any potential trouble that may disrupt the happiness and serenity of Venus. Think of Mars like a bouncer at a nightclub who keeps unruly patrons at bay so Venus can dance the night away. How does Mars remain a peaceful protector instead of becoming enraged and intimidating the patrons? By not taking things personally.

Don't Take Things Personally

Not taking things personally and remaining self-composed can be a herculean task—indeed, it's a job for Superman. In many ways, Superman epitomizes the ideal Mars negative. He has tapped into his Mars energy and channeled it into noble causes—fighting for justice and championing the underdog. Indeed, his Mars has given him an incredible immune system and such superhuman strength that he can leap tall buildings in

Fig. 4.15. Not taking things personally is a superpower.

a single bound and bullets bounce off his chest. And, of course, he never takes things personally or loses his temper.

Now, ask yourself what would happen if Superman took things personally? Well, it wouldn't be pretty. Imagine that Superman is speeding to save a trainload of helpless commuters about to plummet off a damaged railway bridge. Suddenly a group of villains starts shooting at him and calling him names. If Superman took it personally, those bullets and insults would hurt his feelings or make him so angry that he would become distracted from his rescue mission. So, instead of being the unflappable Man of Steel that everyone loves and admires, Superman ends up either venting his rage on the bad guys or pouting and feeling sorry for himself wondering why he was picked on. In the end, Superman's Mars energy got caught in thinking and taking things personally.

Taking things personally allows Mars to act as a malefic influence in our lives. Instead of letting go of hurts, we accumulate them and dwell on them. We may internalize our hurt and become one of the walking wounded. Consequently, we use up our Mars energy by reacting to people and situations with hurt, anger, or aggression instead of maintaining our self-composure. We have to be like Superman and let the bullets and insults bounce right off us so we can arrive at the broken train track to save the day.

Taking Out the Trash

Mars negative can also be compared to a garbage disposal because it can instantly dispose of any negativity that is polluting Venus, just as the device removes leftover food scraps in our sink. But sometimes the garbage disposal breaks down and the waste starts to pile up.

It is important to remember that we can only endure so much negativity. If we hold on to all the hurts we've experienced since early childhood, either real or imagined, the "garbage" begins to pile up and spill into Venus, poisoning our body and souring the sweetness of life. Because we are holding on to wounds from the past, we can be consumed by negative emotions and immediately react to the slightest provocation.

A bulge on Mars negative is a telltale sign that our Mars is due for a checkup. Let's take a look at why a Mars negative bulge ranks as one of the biggest happiness blockers in the hand.

The Battle of the Bulge

Dealing with Negativity on Mars Negative

As Mars negative pertains to our first breath and childhood memories, a bulge on the mount denotes we are holding on to feelings of anguish and frustration that we have accumulated throughout our life. If our hurt stems from early childhood, it is likely we felt we were being treated unfairly at the time, but we were not in a position to confront or overcome our opposition. In other words, we were incapable of standing up for ourselves, voicing our distress, and dealing with our feelings. Hence, we were forced to repress those emotions, which eventually accumulated into a bulge on Mars negative. As a result, we carry this suppressed anger into adulthood, which can manifest as sarcasm, disdain, anguish, unpredictability, and sudden outbursts of negative emotions.

A bulge on the mount signals that we have difficulty letting go of hurts and misunderstandings. On the contrary, we cling to them, inflaming them further with our constant focus and questioning. This results in a tendency to react negatively to anything that frustrates us or anyone we perceive as opposing us.

A bulge makes us extremely subjective, so it is difficult for us to recognize how emotionally reactive we are and how inappropriate and hurtful our words and actions can be.

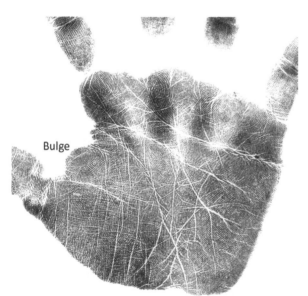

Bulge

Fig. 4.16. A bulge on Mars negative reflects accumulated anguish and frustration.

Learning to observe ourselves and how our behavior impacts others is the first step in deflating our bulge and balancing our Mars energy. As we do this, we will learn to let go of our painful memories and perhaps even look upon them with gratitude for providing us with an important learning opportunity.

One of the best methods to repair our Mars negative is deep breathing.

✶ Deep Breathing: Keeping Mars Negative Balanced

According to Kristoffer Rhoads, PhD, a clinical neuropsychologist, when we are stressed or anxious, our breathing tends to be irregular and shallow, which makes it hard to get air. Breathing deeply increases our air flow, which calms our nerves and reduces stress and anxiety.

Interestingly, Rhoads also points out that a state of anxiety or panic is created by taking short, shallow breaths from the chest. Hence, when we are feeling stressed, deep breathing can calm us down and we are then able to see the world more objectively.

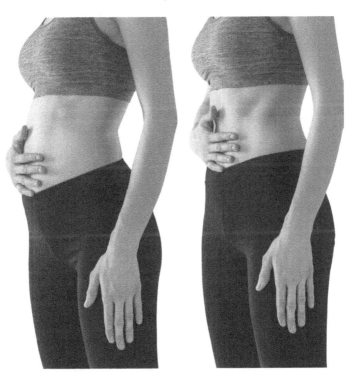

Fig. 4.17. Deep breathing reduces stress and anxiety.

There are two parts of our nervous system—the sympathetic, related to our fight-or-flight response, and the parasympathetic, related to the rest and repair mode. Rhoads says, while "it is not possible to turn the sympathetic nervous system off completely," we can "turn the volume down on it" by shifting our breathing "to a modulated, slow, relaxed pattern."

Indeed, Mars negative instinctively responds to emergencies by triggering the fight-or-flight response of our sympathetic nervous system. When the fight-or-flight alarm goes off, many of our bodily functions are put on pause, such as digestion and blood flow to the frontal lobes of our brain, where creative thoughts take place. However, that alarm is only supposed to go off in an emergency to get us away from danger, which is fine because we can do without digesting food or coming up with creative ideas for short periods. Consequently, while fight-or-flight is necessary to save our lives it should not be maintained for long periods of time.

But the problem today—given the modern dilemma of climate change, social and political unrest, and the twenty-four-hour news cycle—is that we live in a continual state of fight-or-flight, and living under continual stress can seriously undermine our physical, mental, and emotional health. As Dr. Ben Johnson explains in *The Healing Code*, "I have literally had patients die after they became free of their disease because they could not overcome anger, fear, feeling unloved, unforgiveness, or other issues in their lives."

So dealing with our stress in a healthy and productive way is one of the top jobs of Mars negative. Mars possesses the power and ability to quickly deflect any negativity and quickly return us to our parasympathetic system of rest and repair. Indeed, developing a powerful Mars will shield us from even the harshest challenges we can face in life. We see this in the case of Dr. H.

✦✦✦

DR. H'S STORY
A Powerful Mars

Dr. H faced incredible challenges throughout his life. As a young Polish Jew during World War II, he was separated from his parents and spent

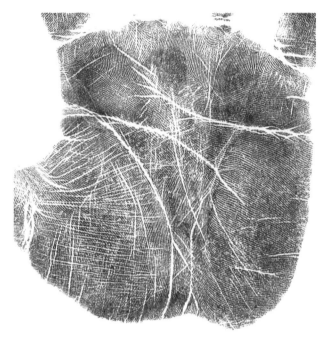

Fig. 4.18. The balanced Mars of Dr. H.

years imprisoned in a series of concentration camps. His father was murdered by the gestapo; his mother died in Auschwitz. When he was liberated from the camps he weighed only seventy pounds. But despite his pain, he maintained his humanity and a desire to help and heal, especially society's most vulnerable.

With that humanitarian outlook, he established a medical practice in Canada after the war and became an outspoken champion for human rights.

Given the enormous amount of pain he experienced, we would expect to find imbalances on his Mars Galaxy that indicated anger, hatred, and a desire for vengeance. Fortunately, his Mars is balanced, and a balanced Mars is imperturbable. It strengthens our nervous system, allows us to deflect negativity, and endows our mind with the power to rise above any challenge. We do not let our problems overwhelm us to the extent that they erode our optimism and destroy our goodwill. Despite what Dr. H lived through during his horrendous childhood experiences, as an adult he was able to maintain his mental peace and serenity and not be distracted from his mission of helping others.

Ultimately, Dr. H was awarded the Order of Canada for his determined efforts to influence Canadian public policy as well as his leadership in the humanistic movement and civil liberties organizations. He lived to the ripe old age of ninety, and before he died said that he was happy with his life.

SUMMING UP THE TRIAD

The health of Venus is dependent on the ability of our Mars to keep us in our parasympathetic system of rest and repair. And the first step we can take in training our Mars to be peaceful and not agitate our Venus is to train our Luna to perceive objectively. The nuclear power that drives Mars should be a neutral force and ideally the mount will only take its marching orders from a thoughtful and reflective Luna; a peaceful Mars warrior begins with a peaceful Luna. Therefore, the combined effect of the triad plays a huge role in our desire to love and be happy and healthy.

Balancing Our Triad

A Long-Term Investment in Happiness

Because they represent the deepest-rooted facets of our personality and our most entrenched character traits, it generally takes longer to see improvements in the mounts than in the major and minor lines. But the good news is that, with some effort, we can transform imbalanced mounts into balanced ones and turn a disharmonious triad into a triad of happiness. We see this in the case of Denise, a much beloved Vedic palmist at the Birla Center.

◆◆◆

DENISE'S STORY

The Case of the Improved Triad

Denise is living proof that a shift in attitude can restore balance to a troubled triad. Before coming to the Birla Center, Denise was an executive assistant at one of the world's largest accounting firms. However, despite the corporate perks—a big paycheck, expense account, luxury apartment, and designer wardrobe—she was miserable. Indeed, she was

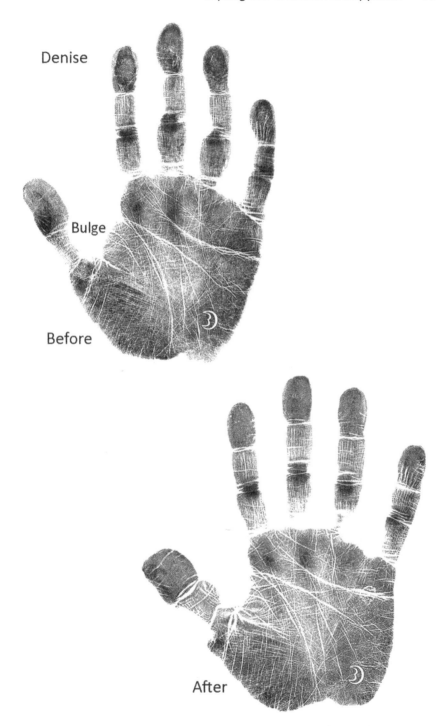

Fig. 4.19. A shift in attitude can restore balance to a troubled triad.

so unhappy that she recalls very little about her first consultation with Guylaine other than crying throughout the entire session.

Nevertheless, after a series of consultations, Denise was able to identify the source of her unhappiness, eventually tracing it to her childhood and having been emotionally and physically mistreated by a younger sibling. She discovered that the pain of that experience had left a deep psychic wound that disrupted her triad, resulting in a shrunken Mount of Luna and a bulge on her Mars negative. Hence, her Luna and Mars were disruptive neighbors to her Venus mount, cramping her ability to be peaceful, loving, and happy.

The fears and anxieties of her Luna, the long-buried hurts, and the reactive nature of her bulging Mars negative kept her constantly on edge. Indeed, she often lashed out at her colleagues at work at the accounting firm. Her supercharged and agitated Mars warrior transformed her diminutive five-foot-two frame into a fearsome presence. She was so reactive that she didn't hesitate to rebuke even her most senior boss. As Paramahansa Yogananda writes in *How to Cultivate Divine Love*, when we act out of anger instead of love, "a woman's three-inch tongue can kill a man six-feet tall."

Denise felt so isolated and alone it was hard for her to picture things getting better; she even began wondering if life was worth living. But then she happened to see Guylaine giving a TV interview about palmistry's ability to transform our lives. Guylaine's words resonated with her so much that she immediately booked an appointment to see her.

The before handprints taken during that first consultation reveal the level of Denise's unhappiness at the time. Indeed, her disturbed triad was reflected by her closed-in fingers, which is a sign of repressed and confined emotions—a major happiness blocker.

Fortunately, Denise was receptive to the wisdom of palmistry. Indeed, what she learned about herself opened her consciousness, allowing her to envision the possibility of living a happier and more meaningful life. She devoted herself to becoming a better person through self-reflection, meditation, and by being of service to others. Instead of lashing out at people, she extended them patience and kindness. In doing so, she tapped into an inner joy that transformed her life.

Within a year, Denise had traded her corporate job for a Vedic life-style and soon became a full-time palmist and counselor. Indeed, her metamorphosis was so dramatic it was as though she had become a completely different person.

This is reflected in her after handprint, in which we see that her Luna has filled out, her bulge on Mars has disappeared, and all **five** fingers are fully open.

The openness of her fingers is especially inspiring. Why? Because, as mentioned, in Vedic palmistry the fingers relate to the five elements of which we are composed. Furthermore, the fingers and elements each correspond to one of our chakras—the invisible energy centers along our spine that, when open, allow us to reach our full potential, connect to our true self, and experience real joy. While we will explore the relationship between the elements and chakras in a later chapter, for now suffice it to say that when the five fingers are open, so too are the chakras. Indeed, the chakras are sometimes described poetically as flowers that blossom when we are feeling happy and productive.

Fig. 4.20. With open fingers, our chakras blossom.

Fig. 4.21. Denise and her husband, Rémi

The closed-in fingers we see in Denise's before handprint mirror the condition of her chakras at that time, which were like wilting flowers. As Denise later said: "My fingers looked lifeless, which was exactly the way I felt back then. But my later prints confirmed how much better I was feeling with all my fingers alive and open."

Today, after happily practicing palmistry for more than thirty years, Denise recalls her first palmistry consultation as a turning point—a U-turn that allowed her to change the direction of her life. She realized that instead of traveling toward despair, she could choose to embrace the path leading to love and happiness.

"What I took away from my reading that day was that I had to stop longing for love and become the love I was longing for," says Denise. "Seeing what Guylaine had done for me, I decided to do the same for myself and others, so I started taking palmistry classes. I focused my full attention on achieving my goal of becoming a teacher and consultant, which led me to meditation and consciously practicing gratitude and kindness in my daily life. I have been happy ever since. The cherry on top is something that I had once believed would never happen . . . I fell in love and married my soulmate."

Denise's happy-ending story is a perfect way to conclude our section on the triad. And now that we have had a good look at the mounts, it's time to turn our attention to the major lines and the role they play in bringing us happiness.

The Harmony of Heart-Head Coherence

If this were a happiness cookbook, which in many ways it is, we'd insist there are two ingredients you can't omit: a peaceful mind and a contented heart—in equal measure!

It is impossible to be happy if our thoughts are troubled, stressed, or fearful. Likewise, happiness will elude us if we are emotionally weighed down with sorrow, a broken heart, little hope, or a lack of optimism. Such maladies of spirit not only block us from being happy but have a negative impact on our physical and mental health as well.

That's why, when it comes to using palmistry to generate happiness, we must always strive to develop heart-mind coherence by balancing our Heart Line (feelings) and our Head Line (thoughts). Indeed, this is so vital to our overall happiness that this entire chapter is dedicated to exploring the relationship between these two major lines as well as the important space between them known as the *quadrangle*. Let's start with the Heart Line.

JUPITER AND THE HEART LINE

Happy Beginnings

The Heart Line reflects our ability to love deeply and unconditionally, which is the cornerstone of a happy life. Indeed, the Heart Line reflects the noblest and most transcendent of human qualities: kindness, empathy, compassion, forgiveness, generosity, and, of course, love.

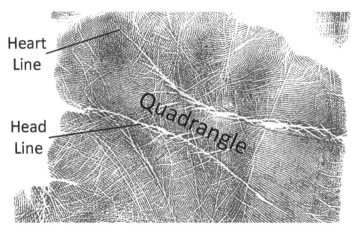

Fig. 5.1. Heart-mind coherence, a key to happiness:
The relationship between the Heart Line, the Head Line,
and the quadrangle between them

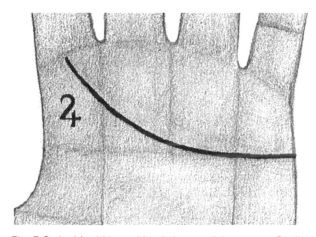

Fig. 5.2. An ideal Heart Line is long, originates on Jupiter,
and travels in a downward curve to the opposite edge of the palm.

Located in the upper region of the palm, an ideally balanced Heart Line is long, originates on the Mount of Jupiter, and travels in a downward curve to the opposite edge of the palm.

Our goal is to have the Heart Line beginning on Jupiter, which allows it to tap into the mount's most uplifting virtues, such as magnanimity, fairness, benevolence, compassion, tolerance, and optimism. A long Heart Line endows us with high ideals; makes us kindly, wise, and loving; and creates such a powerful personal magnetism that people flock to us to bask in our warmth and goodness.

✦ HAPPINESS BOOSTER ✦

Grow a Long, Strong Heart Line

Developing an ideal Heart Line means ensuring it originates on Jupiter. Don't panic if it doesn't originate on Jupiter. We can lengthen the Heart Line and help grow roots that extend to Jupiter by visualizing that the line is actually reaching the mount. This visualization exercise will be more effective if we understand that, before we can embrace true happiness, we must do our best to love others without any strings attached. When we express selfless love—for our family, friends, neighbors, and community—we become magnets of love and draw happy, loving people and positive circumstances into our lives. If your Heart Line is short, meaning it does not originate on the Mount of Jupiter but somewhere nearer to the middle of the palm, try to adopt these famous words from Saint Paul as your personal credo (1 Corinthians 13:4–8):

> Love is patient, love is kind. It does not want what belongs to others. It does not brag. It is not proud. It is not rude. It does not look out for its own interest. It does not easily become angry. It does not keep track of other people's wrongs. Love is not happy with evil. But it is overjoyed when the truth is spoken. It always protects. It always trusts. It always hopes. It never gives up. Love never fails.

Following this simple formula will ensure even the shortest Heart Line will begin to grow longer and develop a gentle curve that reaches into the Mount of Jupiter. How does this make us happier, you ask? Well, as we've discussed, Jupiter reflects an expansion of consciousness through which we not only discover our purpose but also realize that we are connected to every other living being. Hence, we naturally become more considerate, tender, and loving in all our relationships, including the relationship we have with ourselves. And if that isn't a recipe for happiness, what is?

THE HEAD LINE

Thoughts Can Be Our Friend or Foe

The Head Line runs through the middle of the hand, ideally originating on the border between Jupiter and Mars negative and terminating on the border between Mars positive and Luna. It is one of the most important lines in palmistry. Why? Because, as its name suggests, the Head Line reflects our thoughts—and our thoughts determine our attitudes, actions, emotions, behavior, and shape how we perceive ourselves and the world around us.

In the Bhagavad Gita, Lord Krishna cautions his disciple Arjuna: "The head can be our best friend or our worst enemy" (chapter 6, verse 6). When the Head Line is our friend, our heart and mind remain united—we are happy because we are free to pursue our dreams and passions with all our heart; we have peace and contentment of mind. However, when we are guided by faulty thinking, misperceptions, and lack of discernment, our thoughts turn against us and become happiness blockers. This is what the seventeenth-century monk Brother Lawrence meant when he wrote in his classic work *Practicing the Presence of God*: "Thinking ruins everything."

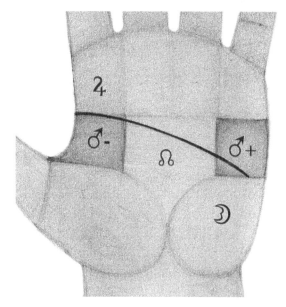

Fig. 5.3. The Head Line reflects our thoughts.

Thankfully, studying the Head Line provides us with a great deal of insight into our mind, and—with those insights—we can adjust our thoughts to pull ourselves out of negative modes of thinking, discover the best of who we are, and create a contented and happy life.

We see how our mode of thinking can either make us happy or miserable in the cases of Cynthia and Meg. Let's start with Cynthia, for whom thinking ruined everything.

CYNTHIA'S STORY

Imagining the Worst

Although Cynthia has a good Head Line, we can tell that she is not using it properly by the web of fine lines crisscrossing her palm, which are referred to as anxiety lines. These lines appear in the hand when our thinking takes a negative turn and begins dominating the way we view our life and the world around us. We are overcome with feelings of anxiety due to either our response to stressful external circumstances or the stress created by our own thoughts and imagination.

A network of anxiety lines shows there is static in our thoughts that is disrupting our focus, robbing us of our peace, and overriding our objectivity. All of this makes it difficult to develop heart-head coherence. In short, we can become nervous wrecks, which is what happened to Cynthia.

Cynthia worked for a major airline where rumors of impending layoffs abounded. Although she was a long-time employee with a flawless performance record, Cynthia convinced herself that her job was on the chopping block. Her imagination literally got the best of her. Every time her supervisor called her name, she expected to be given a pink slip. Her hands trembled and her heart palpitated throughout the day. Fearing a heart attack, she visited the company doctor and was ordered to take stress leave. This only exacerbated her anxiety; she worried that being absent from work made it more likely she'd be fired. Ironically, when she returned to the office, she discovered that her fears were unfounded and, indeed, her boss was considering her for a promotion.

Cynthia's before and after prints illustrate how our thinking can ruin everything. In her before prints, we see her hand is free of anxiety lines, reflecting that Cynthia is channeling her thoughts calmly and productively. In fact, she was enjoying her life and her job. However, when rumors of layoffs began to circulate, negative thinking set in and she began to imagine worst-case scenarios until she literally worried herself sick, resulting in the anxiety lines we see in her after handprint.

Fortunately, Cynthia was able to learn from her handprints and trace the source of her anxiety to overthinking and misperception. She recognized the power of her thoughts and determined to use them more positively in the future.

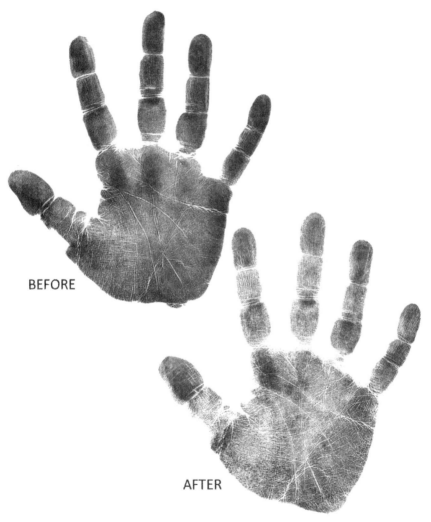

BEFORE

AFTER

Fig. 5.4. Cynthia's before and after handprints

◆◆◆

MEG'S STORY
Letting Go of the Past

Meg is an inspiring example of how we can use the power of our thoughts to overcome hardship, heartache, and any circumstance that blocks us from being happy. Indeed, Meg had a lot to overcome; as we can see in her before print, she has so many anxiety lines covering her palm that it is difficult to even see her Head Line. All this stress in the hand shattered her thinking process, resulting in confusion, jangled nerves, and an anxious temperament.

Meg's problems stem from childhood and her memories of her distressed mother. She recalls many occasions on which her mom dragged her along as she searched every tavern in New York looking for Meg's alcoholic father. These events negatively impacted her mind and weakened her nervous system. As a child, she was plagued by night terrors; as an adult, she has suffered with severe anxiety that has made carrying out her daily duties difficult. For example, even though she earned a teacher's degree, her anxiety prevented her from teaching; indeed, she was so stressed-out on her first day in front of the class, she fainted. That episode was a wake-up call, and although she decided to leave the teaching profession, Meg chose not to let her negative thoughts dictate her life. She calmed her nerves through daily meditation, found

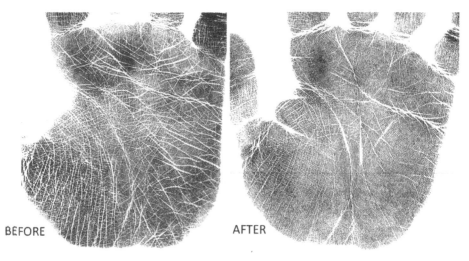

BEFORE   AFTER

Fig. 5.5. Meg's remarkable before and after transformation

fulfilling employment as a community worker, married, and started a family.

We see the remarkable transition Meg underwent by examining her after handprints in which it is difficult to find any anxiety lines at all. Her Head Line is now clearly visible and even has a fork at the end of it, which denotes highly productive creative thinking.

✦ HAPPINESS BOOSTER ✦

Visualizing the Ideal Head Line

When striving for happiness, we need to extend our Head Line so it reaches the border of Mars positive and Luna. This will allow us to tap into the calmness and courage of our Mars warrior as well as benefit from the sensitivity, imaginative powers, and creative energy found in Luna. Taking on these qualities gives us a broader vision of our potential and helps us to go for our dreams. One of the fastest ways to develop our Head Line is through the power of visualization.

Many scientists and sports psychologists say that our brain activates the same neural networks whether we are experiencing

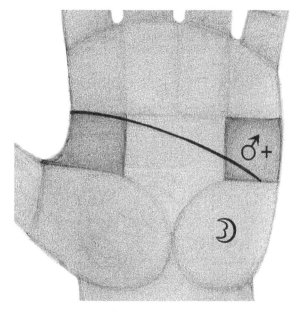

Fig. 5.6. The ideal Head Line

something in the real world or simply visualizing it. In other words, sitting in a hot tub calmly visualizing that we are skating across a frozen ice rink will produce the same effect in our brain as actually going to the rink and getting on the ice. Visualization has been used for years as a training technique by many professional athletes. Arnold Schwarzenegger once said his bulging muscles were produced from 50 percent sweat and 50 percent visualization. Legendary golfer Jack Nicklaus practiced each shot in his mind before he took it. Many of our clients have used visualization to improve the features of their hands.

To extend your Head Line, imagine it as a long, deep, slightly curved line without any breaks or interferences. Look at the picture of the ideal Head Line (fig. 5.6) and fix that image in your mind. Then find a quiet spot where you won't be disturbed and sit comfortably on a chair or couch. Close your eyes and take a few minutes to connect with your breath and be aware of it gently flowing in and out while visualizing your own Head Line growing longer and deeper.

THE HEART-MIND CONNECTION

Happiness through Coherence

Now that we understand what our Heart and Head lines are all about, we can look at how they work together. One of the biggest challenges we face when trying to find, create, and hold on to love and happiness is making sense of the mixed messages we send ourselves when our head and heart aren't in sync. How do we decide who's the boss? Do we listen to what our heart is telling us to do, or to what our head is telling us to do?

Well, as mentioned, there aren't many places in the hand where it is more critical to establish balance than between the Heart Line and Head Line. When our Head Line and Heart Line are out of balance—when our thoughts and heart aren't properly communicating with each other—we can run into big trouble, and fast. A heart-head imbalance can negatively impact us in our daily lives, play havoc with our love life, and hold us back from living a meaningful and happy existence.

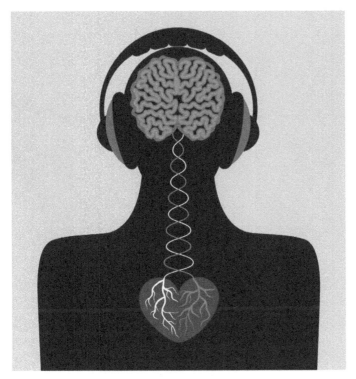

Fig. 5.7. A critical connection:
Heart-head coherence

It's probably easy for you to recall an occasion when you, or some-one you know, has been unable to figure out which signals to follow—those being sent from the heart or head. For example, should you follow your heart and become an artist because you passionately love to paint, or should you take the high-paying corporate job because it offers secu-rity, even though you know you'll hate it and it will probably make you miserable? Do you marry the person who is a real sweetheart and who'll definitely be a good parent and faithful partner, or do you run off with the other person, the one that your mind keeps warning is all wrong for you but who makes your blood hot and your heart race? Do you stay in a passionless marriage because your head is telling you that you'll end up alone, or do you strike out on your own in search of love and self-fulfillment?

These kinds of wrenching personal dilemmas all stem from a lack of heart-mind coherence and are, sadly, as commonplace as they are

Fig. 5.8. The happy marriage of heart and head

painful. It's one of the main reasons we decided to write this book—so we can all learn how to create a balance between our heart and head and ensure we're always acting out of love instead of agonizing over it. When our heart and head are in coherence, we open ourselves up to our higher self and our finest qualities, which makes finding happiness so much easier.

One of the biggest challenges in finding love, happiness, and joy is an imbalance between the Heart and Head lines. Sometimes the problem is with the Head Line, sometimes with the Heart Line. When our Head Line overpowers our Heart Line, our emotions can get shoved into a deep freeze, making our expression of love hard and brittle. When our Heart Line overpowers our Head Line, our reason and discernment get hijacked by our emotions, leading to unpredictable behavior that results in unhappiness.

The quickest way to determine balance in the energies of our heart and head is by checking the quality of the quadrangle in the center of our hand.

The Quadrangle

Delicate Balancing Act of Heart and Head

A well-formed and well-spaced Head Line and Heart Line will produce a lovely quadrangle in the middle of our hand, which is universally considered to be one of the most mystically charged and auspicious formations in palmistry. That's why the space between the Heart and Head lines is poetically referred to as "the landing strip of the angels."

A balanced quadrangle is formed by a long, deep Heart Line (our emotions) and an equally long, deep Head Line (our mind). This is a sign that a powerful and positive connection exists between our heart and

Fig. 5.9. The quadrangle–landing strip of the angels

mind . . . our passion, intuition, and reason are operating in sync; we are emitting, and open to receiving, love and loving energy. The magnetism of a healthy, balanced quadrangle will attract divine blessings into our lives, which often show up in the form of visionary dreams, dear friends, inspired teachers, and soulmates. We see this in the case of Stephen.

◆◆◆

STEPHEN'S STORY

The Happy Healer

Stephen was a renowned holistic healer. The combination of his vast knowledge of Ayurvedic medicine, wisdom, empathy, and loving nature ensured that he had a long list of faithful clients who traveled from across North America to see him. Despite his popularity, Stephen was facing the stress of keeping his business solvent and paying his mortgage.

While the stress of such a situation could have easily overwhelmed many of us by trapping us in either panic or despair, or push us to simply give up, Stephen maintained his composure; he remained upbeat, positive, and energetic.

Fig. 5.10. Stephen's balanced quadrangle

Thankfully, Stephen's well-formed landing strip of the angels attracted many supporters who got together and provided the financial backing he needed to open a new clinic and keep his home.

How did Stephen deal with such adversity with unruffled calmness? Well, in short, by maintaining heart-head coherence, which is reflected in his handprint by the balance between his Heart and Head lines.

✦ HAPPINESS BLOCKER ✦
The Imbalanced Quadrangle

But what happens to us when our quadrangle, our landing strip, isn't quite angel-ready—when our Heart and Head lines are unequal and misaligned? We can get a good idea by looking at the stories of Loretta and Claudia, who each demonstrated a lack of heart-mind coherence in different ways but ended up going down the same painful path.

✦✦✦

LORETTA'S STORY
A Need to Listen to the Whispers of the Heart

Loretta was a well-known and highly respected psychologist and marriage counselor. She'd written a bestselling book on developing successful relationships and was a frequent guest on radio and TV talk shows, where she offered advice to troubled couples. There was no doubt about it, Loretta was intellectually brilliant, possessed an extraordinary mind, and had saved a lot of relationships. However, she was struggling to save her own marriage and keep her family together.

Loretta came for a palmistry reading at the insistence of her husband. He had long complained that Loretta was emotionally unavailable to him and their two school-age daughters, although Loretta insisted that she was doing her best. She was not aware of the emotional toll her remoteness was taking on her loved ones—or herself.

"Hey, it's true that I have a career and I'm busy, but I make sure I'm home for dinner every evening. I'm confused—I don't know what they want from me," Loretta reasoned during her first consultation.

Well, it was obvious what her husband and daughters wanted—it wasn't more of her time, it was more of her love and affection.

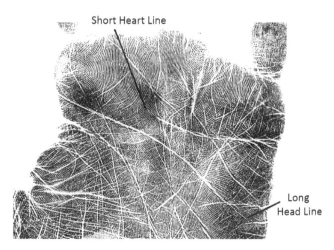

Fig. 5.11. Loretta's imbalanced quadrangle:
The Head Line dominates the Heart Line.

Unfortunately, Loretta's head was doing all the talking and not listening to her heart. As a result, she had no heart-mind coherence.

In her handprints, we can see that her Head Line is nearly twice the length of her Heart Line. In other words, her head is overpowering her heart, creating disharmony in her life. To remedy the situation, she needed to listen to the whispers of her heart, and not let them be drowned out by the booming voice in her head. Loretta needed to grow her Heart Line. And what better place to start practicing love than at home with her loved ones? Hence, it was suggested to Loretta to be more attentive to her husband's concerns and needs, and to make a conscious effort to be more emotionally present with her daughters.

◆◆◆

CLAUDIA'S STORY
A Need to Listen to Reason

Claudia had the opposite problem of Loretta but experienced very similar disharmonious results. Where Loretta's Head Line overpowered her Heart Line, Claudia's Heart Line overpowered her Head Line, which can cause our emotions to run amok.

Claudia was a popular and effective guidance counselor at a veter-

Long
Heart
Line

Short
Head Line

Fig. 5.12. Claudia's imbalanced quadrangle:
The Heart Line dominates the Head Line.

ans' hospital. Her passion and empathy enabled her to help many male and female soldiers returning from conflict zones successfully adjust to civilian life. She'd always managed to maintain a personal connection with her patients while keeping a professional distance. That is, until she fell in love with her patient Patrick. Claudia didn't pursue him and dutifully kept her feelings to herself. But her intense emotional attraction to him eventually overpowered her reason. Although Patrick never displayed a romantic attraction to her, Claudia convinced herself that little things he said and did proved that he loved her as much as she loved him—that they shared a special and mutual bond.

Then one day she saw Patrick and another patient standing together, holding hands and kissing. Claudia was heartbroken and deeply angered at what she perceived to be a blatant, humiliating, and unforgivable betrayal.

Claudia had to realize that her anger had very little basis in reality, as she had never openly shared her feelings with Patrick. Still, she was emotionally distraught, and unable to overcome her rage or allow herself to forgive Patrick. She handed his case over to another counselor and tried focusing all her energy on her other patients, but eventually she lost all enthusiasm for her work and took an extended leave from her job.

Claudia's Heart Line, unsupported by her Head Line, was overpowering her reason and objectivity, causing her great emotional suffering, which also negatively impacted her career.

Eventually Claudia came to realize that Patrick had actually done her a favor by making her recognize that to be happy and love someone the way she wanted to be loved, she must first confront her lack of heart-mind coherence. And that meant she needed to improve her Head Line by becoming more objective and trying to see the bigger picture. She needed to recognize that if a feeling of love could be awakened once, as it had with Patrick, it could happen again, but this time with a mutually receptive partner.

The imbalance in Claudia's Head Line can be corrected by aligning her Heart and Head lines, which will ensure her quadrangle is open to receive loving relationships and positive circumstances that enrich her life and bring her untold happiness.

✦ HAPPINESS BLOCKER ✦
When the Heart Line Disrupts the Quadrangle

While a Heart Line that turns up and reaches the Mount of Jupiter provides us with optimism and idealism, a downward-turning line closes off the quadrangle—the landing strip that draws positive circumstances and kind, caring people (angels) into our lives.

When the entrance of our landing strip is blocked by a downward-turning Heart Line, it impedes the spontaneous expression of our

Downward-turning Heart Line

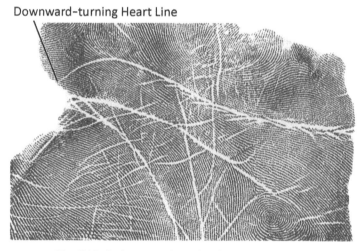

Fig. 5.13. A downward-turning Heart Line blocks
the entrance of our quadrangle.

heart, which is not conducive to happiness. We are preoccupied with examining the motives of others and trying to determine whether or not they are sincere and truly love us. This produces an excess of skepticism and doubt, which, of course, naturally blocks us from being happy.

Constantly worrying about the motives of others squanders energy we could be using to express our love. Hence, we become the architect of our own unhappiness, which is why it is important to keep our quadrangle open by loving as unconditionally as we can.

The good news is that with a little bit of effort, we can all enjoy greater heart-head coherence as we see in the cases of Bruno and Desmond.

BRUNO'S STORY

The Propelled Heart:
Transformation Is Possible

Bruno, a childcare worker, was unhappy in his job as a disciplinary "enforcer" at a reform school for emotionally troubled and violently aggressive teenage boys. Although his Heart Line was short, not reaching Jupiter, he had a Ring of Solomon on Jupiter (a semicircle around the mount)—a sign of wisdom that, as the name suggests, reflects an ability to understand, relate to, and empathize with other people. It's not uncommon to find a Ring of Solomon in the palm of someone working in a helping profession. Consequently, it was suggested that he would find life more rewarding if he changed direction by, for example, counseling the boys in his charge rather than simply disciplining them.

He was encouraged to develop his Heart Line to Jupiter in order to tap into the innate empathy suggested by his Ring of Solomon. This resonated with him as he wanted to get along with people better. He persisted each day visualizing his Heart Line growing. He tried to incorporate all the ideal qualities of a longer heart on a daily basis; for example, he practiced expressing empathy and concern for his coworkers and how the youngsters in his care were feeling. Within three months, he found himself more approachable as people began to relate to him more easily. By allowing his heart to open, he increased his magnetism,

BRUNO

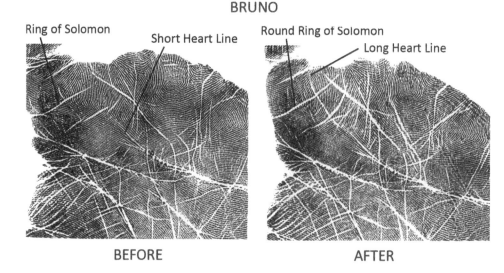

Fig. 5.14. Bruno's after print shows a longer Heart Line and longer, rounder Ring of Solomon.

which is reflected in his after print by his longer Heart Line and longer, rounder Ring of Solomon.

His new attitude and outlook were recognized by others and soon he was promoted to the position of ombudsman at the reform school. This meant he was no longer an enforcer, but a counselor who created greater harmony between the boys and social workers.

◆◆◆

DESMOND'S STORY

Never Too Late for Change

Desmond was a free-spirited jazz musician in his youth but hung up his saxophone when he got married and had children. Being the responsible sort, he traded his musical career for a job in sales. He never regretted taking care of his family, which he deeply loved, but he missed making music and was often preoccupied with worry and anxiety at work and paying the bills at home.

After forty years at the same job, Desmond retired. But instead of sinking into his La-Z-Boy chair and ruminating over what might have

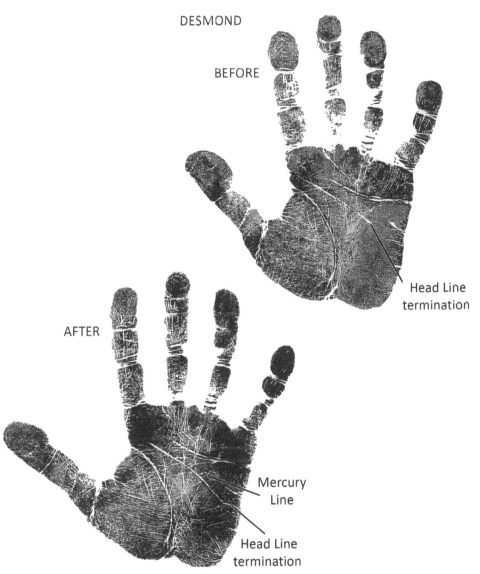

DESMOND

BEFORE

Head Line
termination

AFTER

Mercury
Line

Head Line
termination

Fig. 5.16. Desmond's after print shows a longer Head Line.

been, he decided to challenge his mind, reengage his brain, and resurrect his creative streak. And in the process, he changed his Head Line and changed his life. Desmond enrolled in a slew of activities and classes, from painting and sculpture to courses in languages and gourmet cuisine. He turned his retirement into a personal renaissance, and he couldn't have been happier!

Fig. 5.15. Desmond (bottom) fully enjoying life at ninety

When we compare his preretirement handprint to his postretirement handprint, we can see that Desmond's Head Line has grown significantly, and there has been a remarkable development in his minor line of Mercury—a line associated with creative expression. So not only has he discovered a newfound sense of peace and happiness, he has developed the means to express his joy and creativity. Desmond got to know his Head Line and befriend it, and that relationship filled his life with happiness.

Indeed, as palmistry teaches us, it's never too late for change!

The Science of Heart-Mind Coherence

Our Health and Happiness Hang in the Balance

There is now a significant body of scientific literature highlighting the importance of a healthy communication between our heart and brain. And new evidence continues to surface that confirms our happiness, as well as the length and quality of our lives, is directly influenced by our level of heart-mind coherence. Indeed, one such study conducted by Harold Reich, which is posted on the HeartMath Institute website, demonstrates the profound impact heart-mind coherence has on our thoughts, feelings, outlook on life, and general health.

In laboratory experiments, test subjects who demonstrated a lack of heart-mind coherence, meaning those who exhibited chronic negative emotions such as anger, frustration, sadness, and high levels of stress, displayed poorer heart rhythms than the test subjects who demonstrated a healthy heart-mind coherence, meaning the subjects who consistently displayed uplifting emotions such as appreciation, kindness, love, and gratitude.

When electronically monitored, the actual heart rhythm of those with no heart-mind coherence produced an irregular and jagged wave form, which was associated with depleted cellular energy reserves, diminished physical strength and cognitive functioning, and greater wear and tear on every system in the body. However, test subjects with heart-mind coherence consistently displayed a regular and highly ordered

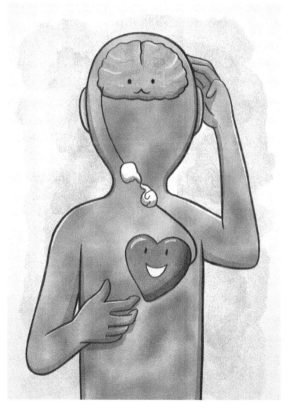

Fig. 5.17. The balancing act of heart-mind coherence

heart rhythm pattern resembling a smooth, harmonious wave, referred to as a *coherent heart rhythm* pattern. This coherent heart rhythm was shown not only to express itself in positive and uplifting emotions but also to chemically synchronize the two branches of our autonomic nervous system—the sympathetic (fight-or-flight) and parasympathetic (rest and repair), improving every bodily function and structure: blood circulation, respiration, muscle endurance, skeletal strength, and cognitive clarity. It also stabilized moods, produced higher levels of the natural "love hormone" oxytocin, and induced an overall sense of well-being. In short, the findings strongly suggest that heart-mind coherence results in a longer, more loving, healthier, and—you got it—happier life!

Finding Joy and Happiness through Meditation

In his book *Breaking the Habit of Being Yourself: How to Love Your Mind and Create a New One*, inspirational writer Joe Dispenza says we can develop greater heart-mind coherence by meditating upon the divine within. He writes that this practice will change our life, and our world, through the sheer force of love: "When you meditate and connect to something greater, you can create and then memorize such coherence between your thoughts and feelings that nothing in your outer reality—no thing, no person, no condition at any place or time—could move you from that level of energy. Now you are mastering your environment, your body, and your time."

Happiness through the Practice of Gratitude

A pastor who used to visit the Birla Center once said that "prayer is the rope that pulls heaven closer to Earth." Well, gratitude is the rope that pulls the heart and head into alignment. The expression of gratitude will help us achieve heart-mind coherence and develop a healthy quadrangle. Why? Because gratitude forces us to both think and feel about the same thing at the same time with the same positive energy. Gratitude brings our heart and head together in a common effort and for a common cause—to unite our reason and our emotion to give thanks.

Practicing gratitude and being actively thankful for the blessings in our lives—be they things or people—will form a balanced communion of reason and feeling.

We have seen in the cases of Loretta and Claudia what can happen when we lack balance between the Heart and Head lines: A war is waged between heart and mind that divides us from ourselves and separates us from the people we care about. Gratitude is the great peacemaker; it allows the heart and head not only to be equal partners but to be the best of friends. But like any friendship, it requires work; gratitude must be practiced regularly to be effective because, as we all know, even best friends can drift apart. So let's make sure to use our head and heart together, and be grateful for all we have.

Many wise and thoughtful people share the fundamental belief that the regular practice of gratitude is one of the surest methods of developing heart-mind coherence, bringing love into our lives, and connecting with a universal feeling of love for all. Eckhart Tolle, author of the bestselling book *The Power of Now*, says: "It is through gratitude for the present moment that the spiritual dimension of life opens up." Darren Weissman explains in his book *The Power of Infinite Love and Gratitude* that gratitude creates a positive channel between the heart and mind (a coherence) that physically removes accumulated energy blockages created by negative emotions.

In short, gratitude creates a harmonious heart-head connection that positively energizes us. So let's add gratitude to our daily to-do list—for

Fig. 5.18. Gratitude pulls the heart and head into alignment.

the sake of a contented heart and a happy state of mind! If you haven't done so already, we suggest you start a gratitude journal.

The good news is that we have the opportunity to improve our heart-head coherence every moment of every day through the way we live and, indeed, with every breath we take, as we shall see in our next chapter, which focuses on the Life Line.

6

Let's Not Forget the Life Line's Role in Happiness

Perhaps no feature of the hand provides us with a better snapshot of how happy we are than the Life Line. As its name implies, the Life Line represents the one thing we absolutely need to be happy—our life!

Indeed, the Life Line reflects our very breath, which transports our *prana*—the life force energy that animates every cell in our body.

The shape, length, and quality of the Life Line not only reflects our attitude toward life but also the way we live. It will tell us if we are happy, joyful, harmonious, or fearful, anxious, restless, or resistant.

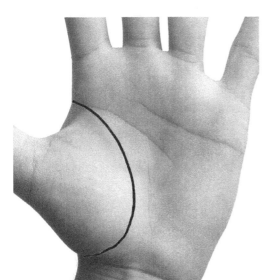

Fig. 6.1. The Life Line reflects our attitude toward life.

The Life Line is also a reflection of our physical health and how much pleasure we take from being alive. Indeed, the Life Line is our pathway to ananda, which we have learned is a state of contented bliss expressed through the feeling of physical joy.

According to the rishis (the divinely inspired yogic seers of ancient India) experiencing ananda is our natural birthright. It is a state of being we can enjoy all the days of our lives. Developing the positive attitude that creates a healthy Life Line is the quickest and surest way to bring joy into our lives. And what is more important than being joyful?

PORTRAIT OF THE LIFE LINE

A balanced Life Line is long, deep, unbroken, and rounded, which is a good indicator of a long, healthy, and happy life. A short, shallow, or broken Life Line is a definite sign we are facing challenges with our physical, mental, and emotional health—and is a signal that we are hav-ing difficulty experiencing ananda.

However, even if we are challenged with a truly troublesome Life Line, there is no need to despair. As we've learned, Vedic palmistry's most beautiful promise is that our lines (and our life) change for the

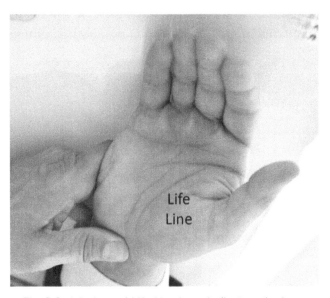

Fig. 6.2. A balanced Life Line is an indicator of a long, healthy, and happy life.

better with a few adjustments in attitude and outlook. Hence, we can change or repair a damaged Life Line, and plug ourselves into ananda, which will give us real and lasting joy.

Perhaps the best thing about having a long and healthy Life Line is that it gives us many opportunities to love and share our love, no matter how many hardships we encounter. We see this in the case of Leona.

--------◆◆◆--------

LEONA'S STORY

A Long, Rounded Life Line

Leona had been in love with her childhood sweetheart for as long as she could remember. They grew up together and swore they would marry as soon as they were old enough, which they did. But shortly after the wedding, Leona's husband died suddenly from a massive heart attack. It was a devastating emotional loss that drained the joy from her life and nearly destroyed her will to live. But instead of surrendering to despair, Leona became more attuned to the human condition. She recognized that her experience was not unique, that many other people suffered from feelings of loss and hopelessness. She made a choice to live life to the fullest and to use her experience to help others.

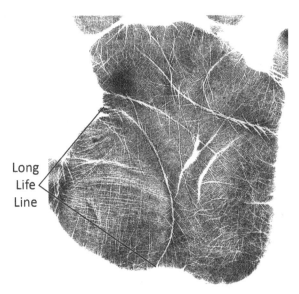

Fig. 6.3. Leona's long Life Line

So, while working nights to support herself and her extended family, she enrolled in university, became a psychologist, and dedicated herself to helping alcoholics and drug addicts recover from their illness and lead healthy, rewarding lives. She quickly gained a reputation as an excellent counselor due to her passion and commitment, as well as her upbeat, caring, and optimistic approach to her clients and to life.

Leona's long Life Line reflects how strongly rooted she is in her conviction that life is a gift that must be appreciated, no matter what. This attitude allowed her to experience the joy of ananda and share that joy with everyone she came in contact with.

The Power and the Privilege

The power we are capable of expressing through the Life Line is virtually indescribable. As Paramahansa Yogananda once said to a disciple who complained about feeling exhausted: "Incredible amounts of energy are hidden in your brain; enough in a gram of flesh to run the city of Chicago for two days. And you say you are tired?" However, because we have so much potential power, we must be mindful of the old axiom that "with great power comes great responsibility." Not only is each of us responsible for how we choose to direct our life force energy, it is our responsibility not to take our life for granted. Being alive is a privilege—a privilege we must honor by making the most of it . . . our life force can flow like a small garden sprinkler or with the full force of Niagara Falls.

The Life Line as a Retaining Wall

Venus and its corresponding finger (the thumb) relate to the element of Earth. Consequently, a long Life Line encircling the Mount of Venus acts as a retaining wall, preventing the element of Earth from eroding and sliding into the neighboring Mount of Luna. And, because Venus represents our vitality, health, and sense of joie de vivre, a protective, encircling Life Line increases our potential for enjoying a long, healthy, energetic, and harmonious existence.

A secure Venus that is firmly anchored by a Life Line encircling it reflects our ability to cope with and weather any storm that arises in the sea of life. When Venus is contained, we are committed to holding fast to its finest and most elevating qualities. We remain steady and consis-

Fig. 6.4. The Life Line acts as a retaining wall.

tent in our love without our focus being sidetracked or our energy being dissipated. The circular journey of the Life Line around Venus terminating at the wrist is an essential part of the path to the joy of ananda.

However, when our Life Line fails to terminate at the wrist—in other words, if it is short or badly broken—our Venus energy is in danger of being dissipated due to feelings of restlessness, the pursuit of excitement, or the escape from the humdrum that can drain our peace and undercut our joy.

◆◆◆

MRS. CULLIN'S STORY

A Life Line Fully Embracing Venus

Mrs. Cullin has a Life Line, and a life force, that just won't quit. At age ninety-six, she is still going strong, leading a happy and healthy life that has provided comfort and joy to countless others for more than nine decades.

Looking at her handprint, we can see that her long, gently rounded Life Line reaches an ideal termination at the wrist, fully encompassing the Mount of Venus. This tells us that the empathetic, nurturing, and loving qualities of her Venus are being channeled through her Life Line. And as we are about to see, those qualities have been expressed in her attitude and actions throughout her lifetime.

Mrs. Cullin, while still in her early twenties, volunteered to serve on the front lines during World War II as a field nurse. For four years, she bravely ignored the dangers of up-close-and-personal warfare to care for hundreds of physically and emotionally wounded soldiers. The courage, empathy, and kindness she displayed on the battlefield earned her many accolades and official commendations.

Her strong, deep, round, and unbroken Life Line is testament to her steadfastness and endurance. It also reflects how powerfully anchored she remains in her convictions even after having weathered many horrific and challenging life experiences. After the war, she continued her work in the healing profession and, in her free time, created homeopathic treatments and medicines that proved so effective people traveled from around the world to consult with her.

Because she has made the most of her Life Line, she has experienced an abundance of joy that she has freely passed along to the thousands of lives she has touched.

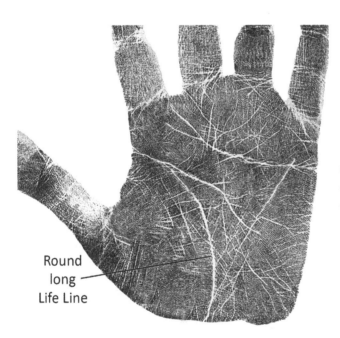

Fig. 6.5. Mrs. Cullin's strong, deep, round, and unbroken Life Line

Round long Life Line

THINKING OUR WAY TO AN IDEAL LIFE LINE

A huge part of successfully creating a beautiful Life Line (and a wonderful life) lies in thinking positively.

Blocking Negativity

We cannot permit any negative thoughts, emotions, people, or circumstances to mess with our head, cripple our confidence, undermine our peace, and generally make our life miserable. When our thinking is out of balance, all of our energies, and just about everything else in our life, falls out of balance as well. And when our life is out of balance, we will find we have a Life Line that is damaged and constricted—a Life Line that is blocking our flow of prana.

✦ HAPPINESS BLOCKER ✦
A Fragile and Obstructed Life Line
Makes for a Fragile and Obstructed Life

We can all be blessed with a Life Line with the length and roundness of Mrs. Cullin's, which both guarantees an unimpeded flow of prana and the opportunity to develop and express the virtues of Venus in our daily life.

How do we do this? By adhering to a healthy lifestyle and keeping a close watch on the quality of our thoughts and emotions. Negative thinking and unhealthy living put us on the fast track to a short, shallow, fragile, and/or fractured Life Line that is pockmarked with obstructions, such as islands, which block the flow of our prana and our happiness.

If we make no effort to address the root cause of those obstructions, sooner or later our life is going to start lurching from one unhappy and painful drama to the next. This was true in the case of Roger.

✦✦✦

ROGER'S STORY
Portrait of a Life and Life Line in Turmoil

Roger's life and Life Line are in turmoil. Looking at his handprint, we can see that the entirety of his Life Line is full of happiness blockers—islands, breaks, fractures, and interference lines. His fragile, weak, and

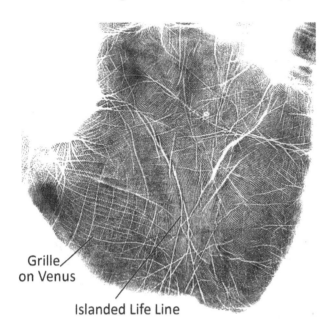

Fig. 6.6. Roger's troubled Life Line

Grille on Venus

Islanded Life Line

broken Life Line is mirrored in his life by his tumultuous relationships, frayed nerves, and emotional and physical exhaustion.

Let's take a look at how Roger's life (and Life Line) took such a negative turn. When we examine his handprint, we see a strong Mount of Venus stamped with a prominent and powerful grille. A grille is a positive marking, denoting a strong desire to love, enjoy life, and live happily. This provided Roger with the incentive and focus to seek out the good life—to surround himself with the best things money could buy. He used his energy and the impetus of his Venus grille to work hard creating his own successful company, which he did, becoming rich and powerful in the process.

However, his grueling work schedule took a toll on his life, his health, and his Life Line. No matter how much his family pleaded with him to slow down and take care of his health, he just kept pushing to get ahead no matter the cost. His compulsive behavior destroyed his marriage and alienated him from his children, leaving him even more physically and emotionally depleted, on top of being guilt-ridden.

When he did decide to take an early retirement and sell his company, he felt alone and lost with his thoughts, with nothing to focus his energy or attention on. As we have learned, a long Life Line reflects a desire to live a long and healthy life so we can fulfill our dreams and share our joy with others. But Roger had no long-term vision to prompt him to live a long and healthy life. He had no Plan B, so when the business was gone, life held little meaning for him.

Roger's grille on Venus and relatively strong Heart Line tell us that he very much wanted to experience the joy of life. But his beaten, battered, and broken Life Line could not channel his energy in that positive direction. When his ideal of a happy life didn't work out, he lacked the physical energy to remain in the fight, and so he just gave up.

Roger, and anyone with a troubled Life Line, can turn toward happiness by connecting to the source of life itself—the universal creative energy of Spirit, to which our soul belongs. That energy is always there within us; it is just a matter of our realizing it by getting out of our head so we can listen to the whispers of our soul. It doesn't matter whether we call this eternal energy God, Spirit, Sat, or the Cosmos . . . when we live in joy, that infinite energy is alive and well within us—we are vibrant, content, and at peace, with no room in our heart to harbor fear, anger, doubt, or regret.

✦ **HAPPINESS BLOCKER** ✦
The Resistance of the Diagonal Life Line

A straight, diagonal Life Line suggests that we are not "going with the flow"—indeed, it means that our prana is following a rigid path, which creates resistance. In physics, the term *resistance* refers to a force that opposes or blocks motion. In our lives, a resistant Life Line impairs our ability to use our energy to create balance, cope with difficulty, and overcome obstacles.

A straight Life Line denotes resistance to and from others as we rigidly cling to our established views and attitudes. It is difficult for us to let go, to surrender, and adapt to the needs of a particular situation. As we are not able to accept life on its own terms—we lack the flexibility to effectively deal with the demands of daily living. And when we resist life and those around us, we unintentionally create even more opposition, exacerbating our situation.

A straight, diagonal Life Line forces us to fight the battle of life twice as hard as others because we make life much more of a struggle than it has to be. Rigidity is the enemy of flexibility, and a straight,

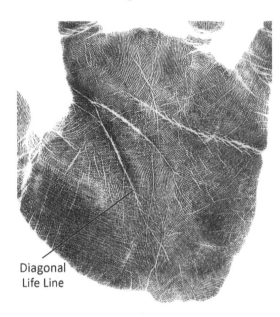

Fig. 6.7. A straight Life Line denotes resistance.

Diagonal
Life Line

diagonal life line can undermine our overall health, our happiness, and the happiness of our loved ones.

◆◆◆

ERIN'S STORY
From Resistance to Flow and Flexibility

Erin is an amazing client who had her first reading when she was just nine years old. Erin's world had turned upside down at the age of two when her parents divorced. The separation profoundly impacted her emotionally and psychologically. Throughout her childhood, Erin manifested her pain and anguish as resistance, stubbornness, and an unwillingness to communicate. No amount of reasoning could convince her to relax and be happy; nothing could persuade her to stop making her life more painful than it already was or needed to be. This is reflected in the straight Life Line we see in her before handprint.

During a consultation, Erin was made aware of the effect her straight Life Line was having on her life. Fortunately, by that time she had grown tired of struggling and was determined to transform her straight Life Line into a round one.

She was inspired by the uncertainty principle of German physicist

ERIN

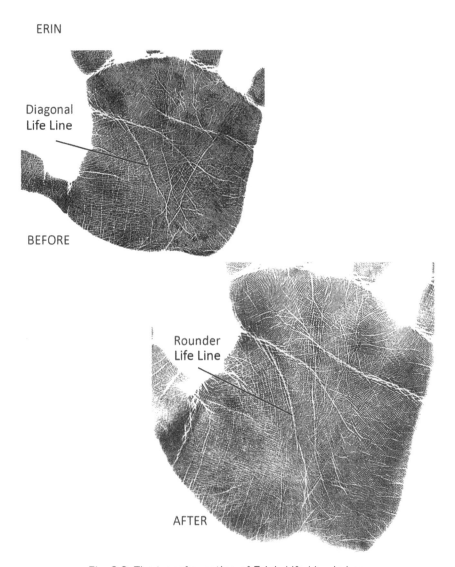

Diagonal
Life Line

BEFORE

Rounder
Life Line

AFTER

Fig. 6.8. The transformation of Erin's Life Line in her
before and after handprints

Werner Heisenberg, which, in a nutshell, contends that when you change the way you look at something, the thing you are looking at changes in response. Erin put that theory to the test by changing the way she viewed the world and her life. And it worked! You can see the incredible change in her Life Line in her follow-up handprints. Indeed, it had been transformed from a straight line to a round one.

She explained that she had radically changed her view of life, and, most importantly, she chose to focus all her energy on being positive. Erin used her energy to transcend her difficult past; rather than holding on to her painful memories, which had made her so unhappy and resentful, she became more flexible. She abandoned her resistance, which freed the flow of her prana, allowing her to use that unblocked energy to create a more harmonious and happy life. In the process, her heart opened and she met the man of her dreams. She also committed herself to helping others discover the same kind of freedom and happiness she had found.

✦ HAPPINESS BLOCKER ✦

Branches to Luna:
The Ho-hums, What-ifs, and Is-that-alls?

One of the challenges facing the Life Line is the strong pull of Luna, which can disrupt the Life Line's ideal course around the Mount of Venus. Indeed, sometimes the Life Line will develop branches that extend into Luna, which we have learned is the mount of imagination. These Luna-seeking branches divert our prana and thereby drain our energy; although they can appear anywhere along the Life Line at any stage of our life, they most commonly develop in the lower midsection of the line corresponding to middle age.

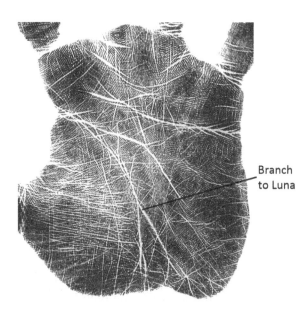

Branch to Luna

Fig. 6.9. Luna branches can disrupt our peace and drain our energy.

Why middle age? Because it is at this juncture in our lives that we may begin to get a sense that there are more years behind us than there are ahead. This may start us wondering: *Is that all there is?* Life may have lost some of its luster, and, even if we have secured a well-paying career, we may sense we are trapped in a rut and approach our work with a ho-hum attitude that leaves us feeling regretful, uninspired, and dreaming of more. The same feelings may creep into our love life—even if we are in a loving, supportive, long-term relationship, the romance and excitement may have morphed into a dull routine; we've grown bored with our partner, and we start wondering: *What if?* What if I had married someone else? What if I were single again? This is when those Life Line branches to Luna are most likely to pop up.

Now, this is a period in our life that can be too often dismissed as a temporary midlife crisis, but it can indeed become a life-ruining crisis if we do not properly act on our restless, disrupting thoughts and emotions. For example, we may suddenly walk out of our marriage or quit our job—giving up something that is truly meaningful, rewarding, and good for us just because we have developed a case of itchy feet. A sudden onslaught of Luna-induced wanderlust can convince us that, by breaking away from our old life, we will feel more alive, and that simply by making a new start, life will somehow be exhilarating and exciting again.

This has happened time and time again with our clients, many of whom have come to regret making major, life-changing decisions based on passing or whimsical emotions. We are not suggesting for a moment anyone should remain in an unhealthy relationship, even if it provides us with a sense of financial or emotional security. Or if your job is truly soul-deadening and utterly quashing your enjoyment of life, make a rational, well-planned decision to find work elsewhere that engages, inspires, and fulfills you.

But it is important not to act on fanciful thinking; instead of impetuously running away from our lives in search of happiness, it is preferable to look within (through meditation, self-reflection, and pranayama) and connect with our innermost self where lasting happiness and joy reside. In doing so, we avoid giving in to escapism, creating needless drama and negative karma, as well as draining huge amounts of life force energy by unnecessarily turning our lives upside down.

Looking inward and changing our life from the inside out will allow us to prune back those pesky Luna branches in a calm and peaceful manner. Getting rid of those branches will stop our prana from leaking toward Luna, fortify our Life Line, and shore up our Venus element of Earth—all of which will help restore meaning and purpose to our life and to the love we have developed and fostered over many years. As Sister Gyanamata, a very wise nun and disciple of Paramahansa Yogananda, often prayed during times of confusion and doubt, "Change me, not my circumstances."

And the good news is, when we change ourselves from within we will see those changes reflected in our Life Line. This was the case with Marcia.

◆◆◆

MARCIA'S STORY

Rescued from Death's Door

Marcia is a perfect example of how we can extend our Life Line by changing the way we think and realizing what a privilege it is to be alive.

In her before handprints, we see that Marcia has a short, shallow, and broken Life Line—in fact, it is almost imperceptible.

There is also a serious imbalance between all three major lines of Heart, Head, and Life—they are not of equal length or strength. Her Heart Line is clearly the dominant major line, followed by a weaker Head Line and, as noted, an extremely fragile Life Line. This imbalance tells us that Marcia's Heart Line is the boss of her hand, and without the balancing influence of a strong Head Line, her Heart Line is dictating the way she lives. Consequently, Marcia is prone to frequent emotional upheavals and lacks the discernment to calm her feelings with reason or logic, which severely weakens her Life Line.

The fragility of her Life Line tells us that Marcia is not grounded or sustained by the element of Earth—the element that supports our body. Because of that, Marcia has a very delicate constitution; she lacks physical strength and endurance.

Although her long Heart Line shows Marcia has a very loving nature, she didn't possess the wisdom to seek a partner who could provide the emotional stability and moral support she so desperately required. Unfortunately, she became involved with a charming but drug-addicted young man who swept her off her feet and got her hooked on drugs as well, an addiction that nearly killed her.

Fortunately, Marcia's palm is graced with a strong Mercury Line, which reflects a deep desire to seek a positive outlet to express herself.

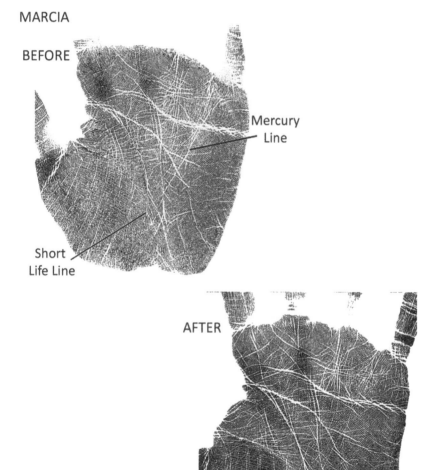

Fig. 6.10. Marcia's before and after handprints

Her Mercury energy kicked in on the night she overdosed. Alone in her apartment and realizing she was near death, Marcia began praying out loud for God to give her a reason to go on with life. At that moment an old friend unexpectedly dropped by for a visit and rushed Marcia to the hospital, saving her life.

With a new lease on life, Marcia swore she would learn to appreciate the precious gift she had very nearly lost. She vowed to no longer be swept away by her emotions and began to look inside to seek meaning and purpose. With that in mind, Marcia started a regular meditation practice, adopted a more nutritious diet, began exercising, and got better sleep. With a healthier and more stable lifestyle, she became less emotionally fragile. She found contentment within herself through meditation and in the growing strength of her body and mind, which led her to the simple, profound joy of being alive.

This is evident in her after handprints, where we see that her Life Line has not only grown but is also much stronger, deeper, and more defined. Her new approach to life is seen in the improvement of her three major lines, which are now equally long and strong. This signals greater overall balance and happiness in her life.

✦ HAPPINESS BOOSTER ✦

Developing Motivational Lines—
We Can Be Inspired Like Ram Dass

The spiritual teacher and inspirational writer Ram Dass devoted his life to leading a harmonious existence and helping millions of others do the same.

This is confirmed by his long, deep, and nicely rounded Life Line that fully encompasses the Mount of Venus and is free of any interferences. But the real telltale signs that he led an inspirational life are the strong motivation lines rising upward from the Life Line. These upward offshoots from the Life Line signal that we possess the power to create opportunities that enable us to realize our dreams and help other people find happiness.

Ram Dass was constantly motivated to move forward with great enthusiasm, hope, and an unceasing desire to move mountains. And he did! Ram Dass donated half the proceeds from a

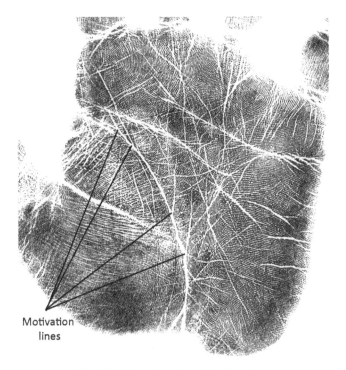

Motivation
lines

Fig. 6.11. Ram Dass's motivation lines

dozen of his bestselling books to humanitarian causes all over the world. At the age of eighty-seven, a year before his death, he published his final book, *Walking Each Other Home: Conversations on Loving and Dying.* Indeed, he led an incredibly productive, purpose-driven, and joyful life, which is reflected in his beautiful Life Line and motivation lines.

Using Ram Dass as an inspiration, we too can grow motivation lines. Our first step in that process should be channeling the best of our Venus through our Life Line by being kind, loving, and compassionate. This will create the magnetism needed to draw positive circumstances and opportunities into our life. When we are receptive to those opportunities, motivation lines will begin to rise from our Life Line, indicating that we are using our life force energy to achieve great things. In short, motivation lines denote we have the initiative to "catch the wave" of opportunity and make the most of it.

Breathing Our Way to Joy

The Life Line is all about the breath, but what do we mean by breath? All people breathe, but breathing does not necessarily enrich our existence or bring us joy. A machine can pump air into the lungs of a brain-dead coma patient, but it cannot enliven them. So, while breathing *is* indisputably essential for life, there *must* be something more. That something else is prana.

As we know, prana is the life force energy that animates our being, fuels every cell in our body, and puts us on the path to ananda. By increasing our prana, we increase our energy and improve our health and happiness. However, as prana is transported through our breath, we have to become conscious of the way we breathe to make the most of our life force.

According to yogic tradition, each of us has been allotted a fixed and immutable number of breaths. When we use up our allotment, our life ends. Since the dawn of history, yogis have studied the manner in which human beings breathe, and for thousands of

Fig. 6.12. Prana: The breath of life

years they have maintained that people whose breath is hurried and shallow inevitably use up their allotment of breaths quickly. However, yogic teaching has also proven that by consciously controlling our breathing—by deliberately taking fewer, deeper, and slower breaths—we can stretch out our allotment and continue living for years, or even decades, beyond the normal human lifespan. This is a truth immortalized in the old Buddhist maxim: "Once you take your allotted number of breaths you die, so use them wisely."

Breath by the Numbers

According to medical research, the optimum respiratory rate for an average adult at rest is approximately twelve breaths per minute. Breathing at this rate supplies the body with sufficient oxygen to regulate blood pressure, maintain heart health, nourish blood cells, and cleanse the organs of toxins.

But most adults in the Western world breathe at a much faster rate—between fifteen and twenty-five breaths per minute. When we are sick, our respiratory rate climbs to between twenty-five and thirty breaths per minute or higher. However, when we are relaxed and feeling safe and comfortable, our breathing slows down, which encourages a strong and healthy heart; clear and focused thinking; and a longer, healthier life.

Indeed, some of India's most renowned yogis—many who have lived in perfect health to age ninety and beyond—attribute their longevity, unfailing photographic memories, and boundless energy to the diligent practice of breath control. From youth, they purposely focus on their breath and slow their breathing—consciously reducing the number of breaths they need to take each minute in order to survive.

This is reflected in the animal kingdom. African elephants, which draw just ten breaths per minute, can live to be more than seventy years of age, and the Galápagos giant tortoise, drawing a mere three or four breaths per minute, has an astounding lifespan of between 150 and 200 years. On the other hand, monkeys and dogs—which both breathe more rapidly than elephants, tortoises, or humans—have shorter lifespans.

Fig. 6.13. Like the tortoise, slower breathing helps us to live longer.

✦ HAPPINESS BLOCKER ✦
Squandering Breath

Unfortunately, most of us are not conscious of our breath; we do not breathe wisely nor with awareness. From the moment we are born, breathing is something we do habitually; we seldom give it a second thought. Without even noticing it, many of us breathe in rapid and shallow breaths all day long. Because we exist in a very stressful world, daily life severely taxes our ability to breathe calmly and slowly. Focusing on our breath can become a low priority when one is preoccupied with juggling the responsibilities of career, kids, mortgages, rising prices, and aging parents.

So how do we become aware of our breath and learn to breathe slowly to boost our prana and create a stronger, longer, and healthier Life Line? The answer is pranayama.

✦ HAPPINESS BOOSTER ✦

Strengthening the Life Line with Pranayama—
Alternate Nostril Breathing

Pranayama is a Sanskrit word that essentially means "breath control" or controlling the flow of prana through the breath. As promised in

Fig. 6.14. Alternate nostril breathing with the nasikagra mudra

chapter 4, we will now take a look at the basic pranayama technique known as alternate nostril breathing.

Before you begin, find a quiet, comfortable place to sit and
make sure you are wearing loose-fitting clothes that allow you to
breathe freely.

The position of the fingers used in pranayama is referred to as
the *nasikagra mudra. Mudras* are hand gestures that direct the flow
of energy. These simple hand positions are easy to do but pack
a powerful punch when it comes to affecting the flow of prana.
Mudras were originally developed by yogis to calm the mind,
restore physical health, and optimize energy systems. Mudras are
codes that the heart, mind, and body pick up on to recalibrate
and rebalance our energies.

You perform the nasikagra mudra by placing the straightened
index and middle fingers of your right hand against your forehead
between your eyebrows. This results in a very relaxed feeling,
helping you to focus and concentrate better on your breathing.
The position of the rest of the hand is as follows:

- The thumb is placed gently on the side of the right nostril.
- The ring finger is placed gently on the side of the left nostril.
- If you find this position difficult to hold for any length of time,
  you can support your right elbow with your left arm.

Fig. 6.15. Finger placement for the nasikagra mudra

Okay, you are all set—get ready to begin a life-changing session of pranayama!

1. Close the right nostril with the tip of your thumb and inhale slowly through the left nostril for the count of five.

2. Then, while keeping the right nostril closed, close the left nostril with your ring finger to prevent any air from escaping through either nostril. Retain your breath for the count of five.

3. Now, open the right nostril and exhale for the count of five.

4. While keeping the left nostril closed, inhale through the right nostril for the count of five.

5. While still keeping the left nostril closed, close the right nostril to prevent any air from escaping through either nostril. Retain your breath for the count of five.

6. Now, open the left nostril and exhale for a count of five.

This completes one round. Try to practice ten rounds each day. Controlling our prana allows us to broaden our horizons, expand our consciousness, and lay claim to the happiness, well-being, and joyful bliss that is our birthright.

- -

Being mindful of our breath and strengthening our prana helps us master our thoughts and emotions, which in turn encourages positive development in our lines, in our mounts, and in our outlook on life.

Mastering Our Inner Energies

The Elements and Chakras

The last several chapters have given us a good understanding of two of the three foundational components of Vedic palmistry—the mounts and major lines—and the role they play in shaping our happiness. However, before we move onto the third component—the minor lines, through which we consciously broadcast our happiness to the entire world—we must dig a little deeper into Vedic philosophy and go beneath the surface of the palm to explore the source of happiness itself: the cosmic energy within us.

IT'S ELEMENTAL
The Five Finger Mounts

Everything in the universe, from the far-flung galaxies of the Cosmos to the humble human body, is composed of the five elements of Creation: Earth, Water, Fire, Air, and Ether.

In the hand, the elements are reflected in the five fingers and their related mounts—Venus ($♀$), Jupiter ($♃$), Saturn ($♄$), Sun ($☉$), and Mercury ($☿$).

THE WHEELS OF LIFE
Our Chakras

Each of the five elements is represented by one of the five chakras located along our spine. The chakras are the body's psychic energy

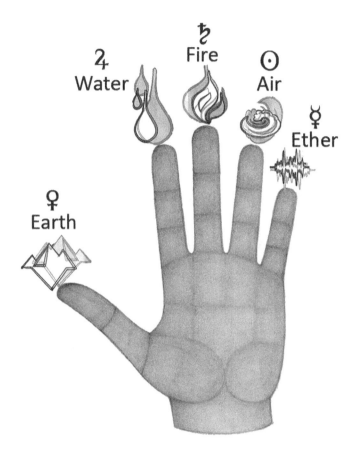

Fig. 7.1. The five elements of Creation

centers. We can think of them as invisible, wheel-like vortices that receive and transmit life energy and help circulate prana. Indeed, they are often referred to as the "wheels of life." When the chakras are balanced and aligned, energy flows freely through them, harmonizing our body, mind, and heart.

On the other hand, imbalanced chakras will have the opposite effect and block the flow of our life force energy, which can result in mental, physical, and spiritual problems. Thankfully, by understanding the chakras, we can easily align and balance them.

There are seven chakras in ascending order from the base of the spine to the top of the head. However, for our purposes in this book, we are focusing on the five chakras that relate to the five physical elements

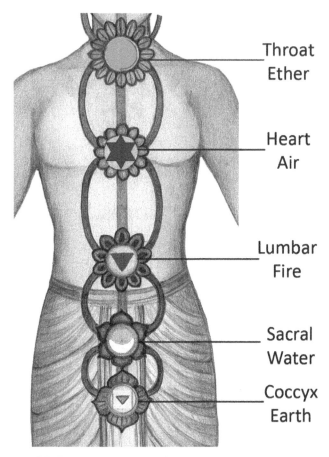

Throat
Ether

Heart
Air

Lumbar
Fire

Sacral
Water

Coccyx
Earth

Fig. 7.2. The five chakras and their corresponding elements

and correspond to our five fingers. They are: the coccyx chakra and the element of Earth, related to Venus and the thumb; the sacral chakra and the element of Water, related to Jupiter and the index finger; the lumbar chakra and the element of Fire, related to Saturn and the middle finger; the heart chakra and the element of Air, related to Sun and the ring finger; and the throat chakra and the element of Ether, related to Mercury and the little finger.

The chakras are like a stairway we ascend on our journey toward happiness and enlightenment. Each step along the way is charged with a specific elemental energy that we must develop in order to embrace and enjoy life to the fullest. Indeed, this is why it is so important to balance our elements and chakras. But to do that requires a basic understanding

Fig. 7.3. Ascending the chakra stairway

of the nature and function of these vital energies and how they correspond to the five fingers.

Let's begin with Venus and the first chakra in the spine, the coccyx.

First Chakra

The Thumb, Venus, and the Earth Element

The thumb and the Mount of Venus (♀) represent the densest element, Earth, and the first, or coccyx, chakra. The flow of this energy has a grounding effect upon us—in fact, in Sanskrit the coccyx chakra is referred to as *muladhara*, meaning "root support." It is the foundation that provides support to all the chakras above it. So it is especially important that the first chakra be as strong and healthy as possible.

A primary role of the first chakra is to deal with issues of survival, security, and stability. The element of Earth provides us with a solid and unshakable foundation upon which we can grow strong and healthy—not only in body but in mind and heart as well.

A balanced coccyx chakra helps us develop strong and stalwart character traits, such as dependability, unswerving loyalty, and

Fig. 7.4. The first chakra

steadiness. However, if we have problems with the first chakra we may become inflexible and rigid, not only physically but in our thinking and outlook on life; we may become stubbornly set in our ways and reject new ideas—a definite happiness blocker when it comes to ascending the chakra stairway toward happiness.

Second Chakra

The Index Finger, Jupiter, and the Water Element

The index finger and Jupiter mount (♃) represent the sacral chakra and the life-giving element of Water. When the second chakra is open, our Water element flows freely. As the seat of our emotions, the sacral chakra is associated with sensitivity, care, and nurturance. It is also our pleasure center where we experience the visceral beauty of life. That energy makes the sacral chakra our source of creative energy. It inspires us to write books, produce symphonies, plant gardens, prepare gourmet feasts, paint masterpieces, build spacecrafts capable of exploring the Cosmos, and bring new life into the world.

Fig. 7.5. The second chakra

Water sustains the element of Earth, enabling it to be prosperous and fruitful rather than arid and rigid. In our lives, the Water element allows us to be flexible in our outlook and attitude.

In Sanskrit, the sacral chakra is called *swadhisthana*, meaning "the dwelling place of the self." Our water chakra nurtures our burgeoning sense of self and encourages it to savor all the world has to offer. Indeed, Water is associated with our sense of taste, which allows us to experience life in all its many flavors. Because they are a powerful source of our individual creativity, the sacral chakra and element of Water help us to find our purpose and leave our unique mark on the world.

Our Water element can be as vast as an ocean or as tiny as a puddle; but either way, that Water has a boundary, be it a shoreline or a rain gutter. We can't get stuck in the sacral chakra because, as we know, if water doesn't flow, it becomes stagnant. Hence, we must ensure that our Water element is free-flowing by being sensitive and adaptable in our outlook and attitude. This will bring out the best of Jupiter, which is an expansion of our awareness.

Third Chakra

The Middle Finger, Saturn, and the Fire Element

The middle, or Saturn (♄), finger represents the element of Fire and the lumbar chakra—the darting nature of Fire makes Saturn the longest finger in the hand. Fire is a transformative energy; in the body it transforms the food we eat into fuel for our cells—it gives us the discipline and sense of responsibility to overcome inertia and get out of bed in the morning. On a more metaphysical note, the element of Fire helps us to transform ourselves into more wise and discerning beings—it is the flame that burns away obstacles preventing us from seeing and embracing the truth. It pushes us to be self-reflective and meditate to develop a clearer understanding of our life and its meaning.

The Fire element not only enables us to see the truth, it helps us to assimilate what we see without getting bogged down by it. In other words, we are able to surrender to the moment by letting go of past hurts and injustices. We are able to forgive both ourselves and others, and instead fill that space with understanding and compassion.

Saturn's primary role is that of a teacher who uses our experiences

Fig. 7.6. The third chakra

to develop greater depth and realize the difference between right and wrong, instilling in us a love of justice, patience, and honesty—which are virtues as precious as gems. Indeed, in Sanskrit the third chakra is referred to as *manipura*, meaning "city of gems." Saturn wants us to be truthful in all we do and especially to be true to ourselves. If we resist the lessons Saturn is trying to teach us, we will create even greater problems and obstacles for ourselves until we learn what we have to learn.

Saturn as Father Time

No matter how unpleasant Saturn's tests may seem, we still want that energy in our life. Why? Because in Vedic mythology, as the Lord of Karma and Justice, Saturn reminds us of the responsibilities and commitments that give meaning to our life.

If you are hoping for a little reprieve from Saturn's taskmaster approach, it is wise to remember Saturn is ever present in our lives. Indeed, numerous cultures refer to Saturn as Father Time, so while we

Fig. 7.7. Saturn as Father Time

may want to avoid its lessons, we can run but we cannot hide—time will always find us out.

In this regard, the planet Saturn is helped out by the hand. As mentioned, the Saturn finger is our longest finger, which means that it is thorough, slow, and patient; it's in no hurry for us to learn the lessons it has to teach. We cannot escape our responsibilities because Saturn invites all of the experiences it wants us to learn right to our doorstep. So it's only a matter of time before we must confront and master the lessons of Saturn. We see this in the story of Immaculée Ilibagiza.

———————————————— ✦✦✦ ————————————————

IMMACULÉE ILIBAGIZA'S STORY
Saturn and the Power of Forgiveness

Immaculée was a twenty-four-year-old university student in Rwanda when the genocide erupted there. She spent three months hiding in a neighbor's tiny bathroom as more than a million of her countrymen, including her friends and family, were hacked to death all around her.

At first, Immaculée cowered in fear as the killers hunted for her; her heart was filled with hatred and hungered only for revenge against those who had mercilessly slaughtered her loved ones. But, as she recounts in her inspiring memoir, *Left to Tell: Discovering God Amidst the Rwandan Holocaust*, "Through deep contemplation and prayer, I came to realize that by continuing to hate, there would be no room in my heart for love . . . not ever again. The only way I could ever hope to invite love back into my life was by ridding my heart of hatred, and the only way I could do that was by forgiving those who had murdered my family . . . and so I forgave them. If I hadn't forgiven, my heart would have turned to stone."

Immaculée had learned what Martin Luther King Jr. had learned and repeated many times: "Darkness cannot drive out darkness; only light can do that. Hate cannot drive out hate; only love can do that."

Saturn offers us the choice to let go of our anger and forgive or to hold on to it and continue to hate. The first choice carries us from Saturn to the Mount of Sun and the joy of our heart chakra. The second choice keeps us stuck in Saturn, going over the same old painful lessons. And who wants to do that?

Fig. 7.8. Immaculée Ilibagiza (*left*)
with Pope Francis

So if, like Immaculée, we want to avoid our heart turning into stone, we must make sure not to get stuck in the manipura chakra and be consumed in its Fire. A healthy Saturn is like a nicely baked loaf of bread. When the oven temperature is just right, our bread will rise perfectly cooked. However, insufficient heat will leave us with a pile of soggy dough, and an overheated oven will leave us with a burnt and crispy loaf. So, ideally, Saturn will burn with a warm and even Fire that sustains and illuminates us. When this is the case, we can use the manipura chakra as a stepping stone to ascend to the heart chakra, the bridge we must all cross on our journey to fully open our heart and experience joy.

Fourth Chakra

The Ring Finger, Sun, and the Air Element

The ring, or Sun (☉) finger, represents the element of Air and the heart chakra, referred to in Sanskrit as *anahata*. Air symbolizes freedom: it cannot be contained, it is not weighted down, and it is untouched by gravity.

Having gone through the fires of the manipura chakra, we have so profoundly committed and pledged ourselves to something that even the most trying of Saturn's tests could not stop us from reaching and embracing the Sun. It is that unconditional dedication that opens the gates of our heart with the force and power of love. We have proven ourselves to be undefeatable, which is why the Mount of Sun is the mount of success.

We persevere because we love whomever or whatever it is that we have chosen to dedicate and commit ourselves to. And that is why, when our Sun is engaged, we are charismatic. We feel whole and complete in ourselves because we are engaging both our mind and heart. So, like a physical magnet, our positive and negative poles are united. Hence, we reach the Sun with a highly charged personal magnetism that radiates with the power of the Sun itself. That magnetic force is virtually unstoppable in its ability to draw success, prosperity, and love into our life.

Fig. 7.9. The fourth chakra

We can all tap into the inner brilliance of our Sun energy simply by being our authentic self and being passionate in whatever we do. This will connect us with our heart chakra, which infuses our being with love. And because the heart chakra is associated with the element of Air, our love has the potential to be boundless. Indeed, our love is constant and offered freely to all. The Sun is impartial; it shines equally on the cauliflower and the cucumber.

The Rocky Road to Happiness:
Reaching the Mount of Sun

The road to the Mount of Sun and its associated heart chakra can be a long and arduous one, but it is a journey that is well worth the effort. To get to this juncture, we passed through the first chakra related to our primal desire to live; then on to the second chakra, where we found our sense of purpose; followed by the third chakra of duty and discipline.

However, a life of duty and responsibility alone can make for a rather bleak existence. So how do we infuse our life with a bit of color and joie de vivre? By getting our Saturn to knock on the door of its neighboring Mount of Sun and open the heart chakra, which will fill all our duties and tasks with love and joy. We see this in the case of Adam.

◆◆◆

ADAM'S STORY

Coloring His World,
Transforming Duty into Joy

One of the happiest people we've ever known at the Birla Center is Adam, a janitor at a large law firm. Adam's job involved polishing thousands of floor and wall tiles every day. Some people may have found that work to be unbearably tedious, but not Adam. He said that each tile he polished reflected his joy because his job enabled him to support his family and put his nephew through college. Adam allowed his Saturn sense of duty to knock on the door of his heart chakra.

From a Vedic perspective, this process is known as turning *gyana*, or knowledge, into *guna*, or virtue.

Fig. 7.10. Adam, finding joy in his work

Turning Gyana into Guna:
Feeling Is the Key

In order for us to turn gyana into guna, we must assimilate the knowledge we've acquired into our character as virtue. In essence, this means that we don't just "know" what the right thing to do is, we feel it in our bones—it has become part of who we are. For example, we know offering our seat to an elderly person is the polite and socially expected thing to do.

However, by connecting with our Sun energy, we can actually feel what the other person is going through, and we offer up our seat to ease their discomfort. In other words, our mind (knowledge) is united with our heart (virtue). We do good out of the goodness of our heart, not because it's expected or because we want people to see us as being kind and generous. No, converting gyana into guna requires both an open and a humble heart.

Fig. 7.11. Turning gyana into guna: Feeling is the key.

Humility is the path to empathy because we are learning to put the welfare of others ahead of our own. We are acting out of the heart, which is fueled by the energy of Sun—the energy of compassion and love. The question, of course, is how do we develop humility? It's a question Saturn will answer for us.

Saturn teaches us humility by bringing us to our knees, either through the pain of experience or seeking wisdom gained through self-introspection. Either way, our ego is pulverized until all that remains is heart. We learn to love and empathize with others rather than judging, criticizing, or disliking them. And as Saturn is related to the sense of sight, both physical and metaphysical, it gives us the ability to see beyond others' character flaws and recognize the eternal beauty of their soul.

Turning gyana into guna carries us forward on our journey; it denotes that we have reached the Sun and are fully embracing our heart chakra, radiating with feelings of compassion and love.

The Element of Air, the Heart Chakra, and the Power of Touch

Even though the element of Air is contained within the atmosphere, beyond which is space, it exists everywhere on Earth. Thus, to our

Fig. 7.12. The heart chakra is associated with empathy and compassion.

mortal selves, it seems limitless with no easily definable borders. Air relates to the quality of omniscience, openness, and conscientiousness of heart. When our Air element is flowing freely, we recognize the goodness in the hearts of others. There is no limit to the expression of our heart; we have the capacity to love deeply and touch the hearts of others. Indeed, the Sun is associated with the sense of touch.

The boundless element of Air operates on every level of existence, from the macro to the micro and everything in between. On a physical level, Air keeps everything in our body moving. It transports our food, oxygenates our blood, fuels our brain, fills our lungs, and keeps our heart pumping. Indeed, air conveys the life force energy of prana to every cell in our body via the breath.

On a societal level, using our Air element makes us influencers—we inspire others to work for the common good; indeed, we are capable of moving mountains for the betterment of humanity. When we activate our Air element, we come up with brilliant ideas, we find solutions to things, we share our light with others, and want to relate with them on a very heart-to-heart, genuine level.

However, as Air is still confined to the atmosphere, our own Air element is also capable of confinement. This happens whenever we put conditions on our love and place expectations upon others—even if our expectation is just to be treated with sincerity and kindness.

When we are being generous, kind, and have good intentions, we can come to expect the same from others. But when we feel let down and disappointed, we can quickly and painfully become crestfallen. The beauty and power of the Sun is that it shines with a pure, sincere, and open heart—however, that is also its greatest vulnerability. No one falls harder than a disappointed Sun.

So how does our Sun energy and big, vulnerable heart deal with painful disappointment? Well, we must keep our Sun-related Air element circulating freely by not placing any restrictions on the expression of our heart. But to do this, our Sun needs to knock at the door of its neighbor, Mercury. As we have learned, Mercury is the mount of transcendence, and it allows us to detach from expectations placed on others. When we experience a taste of the joy that this detachment brings us, it makes room in our heart for our empathy and compassion.

Fifth Chakra

The Little Finger, Mercury, and the Ether Element

The little finger, or Mercury (☿) finger, represents the element of Ether, the most refined of the five elements. The fifth chakra is often referred to as the throat chakra, relating to communication. The throat chakra, known in Sanskrit as *vishuddha*, is all about self-expression in every conceivable form, be it speaking, listening, writing and reading, singing, dancing, using sign language, producing computer code, passing along our genetic code in DNA . . . or sending messages telepathically.

Ether is the original element of creation—it is through ether that all other elements and everything in the physical universe came into existence.

While ether is one of the five physical elements, it is fundamentally different from the other four elements as it exists beyond normal physical constraints; for example, it is neither bound by gravity nor confined by the atmosphere. It is the subtlest of the elements and exists on the threshold between the visible and the invisible; it is indiscernible to the human eye but is all pervasive; it encompasses both the organic and inorganic; it is immaterial but gives shape and form to all matter; it is the source of matter and the space in which matter exists. And it is

Fig. 7.13. The fifth chakra

the bridge between the worlds of the manifested and unmanifested—between matter and Spirit.

In addition to the gift of hearing and speaking, the element of Ether relates to intuition, the "subtle voice" that we hear internally when we have a gut feeling about something or act on a hunch. An exceptionally fine-tuned Ether element can even provide us with the gift of telepathy, the mental transference of thought, and the power of clairaudience, the ability to receive thoughts or messages that are not heard by our physical ears. Think of Beethoven, who wrote his Ode to Joy masterpiece when he was deaf. The more developed our Ether element, the easier it is for us to express our gifts, talents, and authentic selves.

The Ether Enigma:
Everything and Nothing

The yogis of ancient India referred to Ether as *Akash*, a Sanskrit word that translates as "space" and refers to both inner and outer space.

Consequently, Ether has no barriers or boundaries of any sort: it fills the cosmic void; it surrounds and passes through planets, stars, and people; it even occupies the microscopic distances between atoms and subatomic particles. Indeed, the Vedas tell us that Ether is the medium through which our thoughts travel, and that the Akash retains a record of every creative thought, concept, and idea humankind has ever had or ever will have.

The Akashic Records:
Accessing the Wisdom of the Ages

This amazing compendium of knowledge is known as the Akashic Records, which each and every one of us can access through our Mercury energy. As we have mentioned, the Mercury-Akash connection is a tremendous source of inspiration for artists, philosophers, and scientists. For example, Michelangelo was obviously connected to the Akash

Fig. 7.14. Michelangelo creating David

when he created his divine masterpiece *David* from an unattractive slab of rough marble. When asked how he did it, he replied that he could envision David within the rock and all he had to do was chisel away everything that was preventing the world from seeing David's eternal, inspiring, and divine beauty.

Many modern-day poets, writers, and musicians don't even realize they are tapping into the Akash when they produce incredibly inspiring works. Indeed, they often say that they were inspired by their muse. Connecting to the Ether—our personal muse—requires that we develop our powers of intuition. We do this by listening to our inner voice, a skill we naturally develop through self-reflection and meditation.

Ether: Our Path to Empathy

Our connection to Ether gives us an intuitive ability to sense how other people are feeling. And because we are in tune with the wisdom of the Akash, we can become true empaths; we are attuned to the pain of others and are able to ease their suffering with our healing vibration, even from a distance. Mercury's association with healing dates back millennia; indeed, the symbol of the Roman god Mercury, the caduceus, is still used today as an emblem of the medical profession.

Fig. 7.15. The caduceus, the symbol of healing

◆◆◆

ELENA'S STORY
Miraculous Metamorphosis:
The Importance of Harmonizing Our Elements

Elena is a joyful, talented, and highly creative woman whose happy and open heart, free and generous spirit, loving nature and beautiful artwork both move and inspire her many fans and admirers. But this wasn't always the case, which we can see in her handprints taken in 2016 (see fig. 7.16 on page 166).

Indeed, her 2016 prints reveal that Elena's Mount of Saturn is encircled by a Ring of Saturn (see pages 212–13) reflecting a deeply sad state of mind that denotes a sense of mental and emotional claustrophobia that has left her feeling closed in, frustrated, uptight, and alone. This is because when Saturn's fiery, transformative energy is not free flowing, it can become malefic and turn against us. We do not want to see any sign or marking on the mount that confines or traps our Saturnian energy. Let's examine the reason Elena developed such a challenging marking.

As a child, Elena felt her mom did not accept her, causing her to feel emotionally frozen, isolated, and distrustful of anyone around her. As Elena herself explained, "when your mom doesn't embrace you and your family is uncomfortable around you, you feel like an alien in your own home. You start questioning and doubting everything and turn inward to escape the pain, which leaves you feeling even more cut off and alone."

Her bottled up Saturn energy negatively echoes across her palm. In her before print, all her questioning, doubt, and mistrust are reflected in her held-in fingers, which denote that her five chakras and five elements are shut down. Furthermore, her held-in thumb tells us that her Venus, the mount of love, is confined, making it difficult for Elena to trust, open up, let go, and spontaneously express love.

However, within a few years, all that had changed. Indeed, the changes we see in her 2024 handprints are truly extraordinary. They reflect a great deal of joy, creativity, and spontaneity. The first clue to her newfound sense of happiness is the openness of all her fingers. When the fingers are open, our elements and chakras are healthy, fully

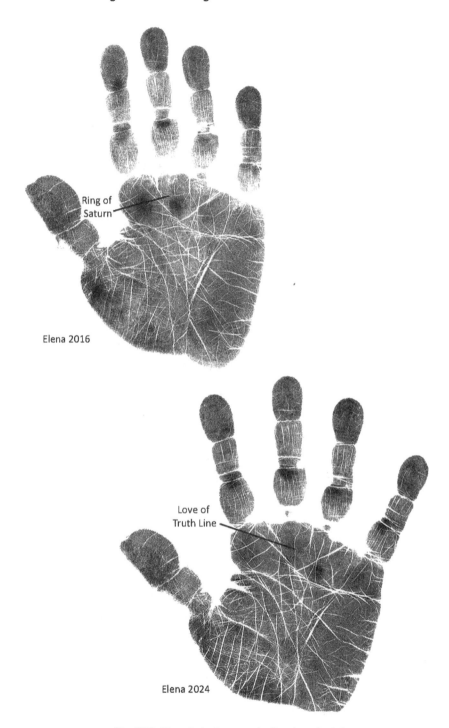

Fig. 7.16. Elena's before and after handprints

ignited, and functioning harmoniously. Her open thumb tells us that her Earth element is strong, making her feel more secure; her open Jupiter finger tells us that her Water element is flowing freely, allowing her to embrace the sweetness of life rather than the bitterness of the past; her open Saturn finger tells us that her Fire element is transforming her painful life experiences into inspiration; her open Sun finger tells us that her Air element is fueling her with creativity and charisma; and her open Mercury finger tells us that her Ether element is connecting to the Akash, supercharging her power of self-expression and providing her with a tremendous sense of inner satisfaction. Indeed, she is filled with a new belief in herself and the power of love. As a result, her creativity blossomed a hundredfold and she began receiving invitations to show her art in galleries around the world.

So you are probably wondering what Elena did to bring about this incredible metamorphosis! Well, it all began when she signed up for a palmistry class at the Birla Center and started to develop a greater sense of awareness. She also enrolled in a meditation course with Paramahansa Yogananda's Self-Realization Fellowship. With the wisdom she acquired through study and self-reflection, she was able to put her past in perspective and be grateful for all the good she could now perceive in her life. Thanks to this inner awakening, her Ring of Saturn faded and was replaced by a Love of Truth Line (see pages 209–10), showing she has come to trust in a divine presence guiding her life.

✦ HAPPINESS BOOSTER ✦

Harmonizing the Elements and Chakras through Our Motor and Sensory Organs

Each of our five fingers corresponds to a sensory organ, which receives information, and a motor organ, which relays information.

Specifically, Earth relates to the sensory organ of the nose and the motor organ of the anus; Water relates to the sensory organ of the tongue and the motor organ of the genitals; Fire relates to the sensory organ of the eyes and the motor organ of the feet; Air relates to the sensory organ of the skin and the motor organ of the hands; Ether relates to the sensory organ of the ears and the motor organ of the mouth.

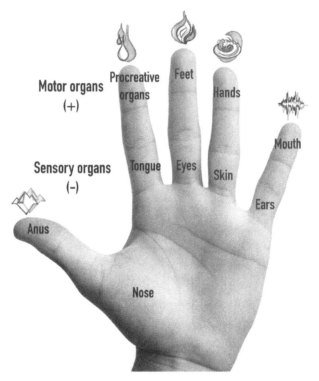

Fig. 7.17. Each finger corresponds to a sensory and motor organ.

In order for our elements and chakras to be balanced, we must develop equilibrium between the incoming and outgoing flow of our sensory and motor organs. For example, to balance our element of Ether related to our incoming sensory organ of ear and outgoing motor organ of mouth, we have to pay attention to what we hear and what we say. Here's a quick way to balance each of our elements and chakras by optimizing the way we use our senses.

- To create equilibrium in the Venus-related Earth element and coccyx chakra, keep physically fit and eat nutritious food.
- To create equilibrium in the Jupiter-related Water element and sacral chakra, simply savor the beauty of life and seek joy through the creative process.
- To create equilibrium in the Saturn-related Fire element and lumbar chakra, develop a long-term vision and endeavor to be open-minded.

- To create equilibrium in the Sun-related Air element and heart chakra, keep an open heart and take joy in other people's happiness.
- To create equilibrium in the Mercury-related Ether element and throat chakra, listen with compassion and speak kindly.

Now that we are familiar with the cosmic energies of happiness at work within the elements and chakras, we are ready to see how these energies manifest in our hand and in our life, which they do through the minor lines—the lines of happiness. We dedicate our next chapter entirely to the minor lines.

Mindfulness
and the Minor Lines

In a word, minor lines are magnificent; they are true beacons of happiness in the hand. Why? Because minor lines appear in the palm when we become consciously aware of our natural gifts, talents, inclinations,

a) Destiny Line
b) Sun Line
c) Mercury Line
d) Girdle of Venus

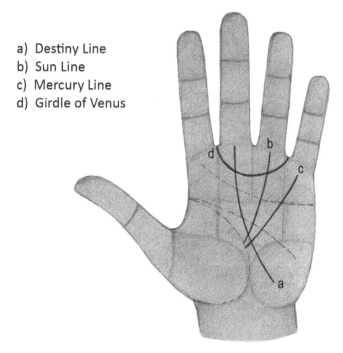

Fig. 8.1. The "Big Four" minor lines

and purpose. Indeed, that's why minor lines are often referred to as "conscious lines." When we find minor lines in the hand, we know that we are tapping into the energies of our mounts, chakras, and elements and expressing those happiness-inducing energies in our daily life. Once we are aware of the relevance of the minor lines, we can take steps to develop them.

In this chapter, we will be looking at the "Big Four" minor lines—the Destiny Line (Saturn Line or Line of Karma), the Sun Line, the Mercury Line, and the Girdle of Venus. The appearance of a minor line signals the blossoming of the attributes connected to the particular finger mount with which that line is associated. For example, the presence of a Mercury Line signals that we are consciously expressing the positive attributes of the Mount of Mercury, the element of Ether, and the throat chakra. Thanks to this, we are able to effortlessly communicate our thoughts, express our ideas, and pick up on the thoughts and needs of others.

Let's begin our exploration of the Big Four with the Destiny Line.

DESTINY LINE
Taking Command of Our Happiness

The Destiny Line is one of the most powerful lines in palmistry. Why? Because its destination in the hand is the Mount of Saturn, with its taskmaster sense of discipline and its driving element of Fire. And because Saturn forces us to deal with our karmic obligations, the Destiny Line imbues us with a powerful sense of purpose. So if you want to live your life without letting the attitudes or actions of others bring you down or distract you from your goals and dreams, grow a Destiny Line!

Indeed, many mental health experts tell us that having a purpose is the key to a long and fulfilling life. When we have a sense of purpose, we are less distracted by daily events and potential stressors. It's not that we don't face those challenges (getting stuck in traffic or an argument with a loved one), but because our attention is focused on a goal, we cannot afford to let it ruin our day or distract us from our long-term vision.

Dedicating ourselves to a unique purpose anchors us; we are better prepared to relate with others based on the fundamental strength

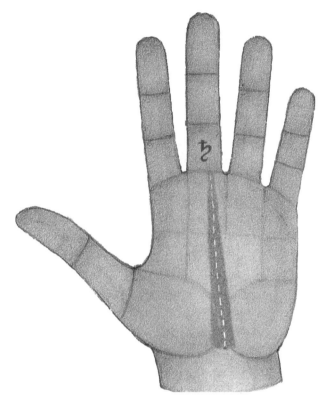

Fig. 8.2. The Destiny Line

of our own character. The presence of a Destiny Line obliges us to use our energy to remain laser-focused with determination, endurance, willpower, and the discipline to stay the course and fulfill our responsibilities.

Striving, Seeking, and Never Giving Up

In many ways, the Destiny Line is like Odysseus—the hero of Homer's ancient saga *The Odyssey*—who, despite distressful decades of war, shipwrecks, and being lost at sea, never abandons his quest to get back to his home and family. Our Destiny Line reflects the journey of our entire lifetime as it travels from the base of the hand, past the Head and Heart lines, to its final home on the Mount of Saturn. Like Odysseus, we may also encounter many challenges and temptations that can prevent us from achieving our goals. To safely sail to Saturn, we must constantly exercise our willpower and discernment to not be pulled off track.

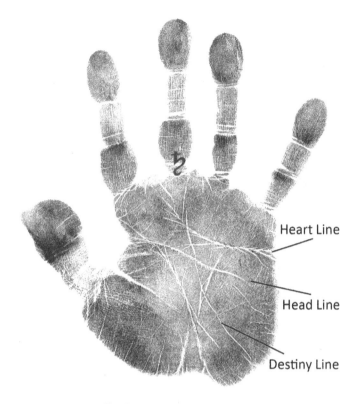

Heart Line

Head Line

Destiny Line

Fig. 8.3. The Destiny Line helps us stay on track.

When we don't have a strong focus on something, a sense of responsibility or dedication, we can easily be disturbed and distracted, which scatters our energy and keeps us drifting aimlessly. This was the case with Robert.

♦♦♦

ROBERT'S STORY
Making a Commitment:
Developing a Destiny Line

In Robert's before prints, we see little activity in his hand other than the three major lines. Robert was living aimlessly without any sense of direction or responsibility; he was not interested in exploring or developing his natural talents or creating a plan for the future. At twenty-eight, Robert was still living at home, without any interest in finding a job, going back to school, or joining the family business.

Adding further pressure to the situation, Vanessa, his girlfriend, was insisting that he make a commitment to her. After a year of in-depth palmistry readings, Robert grew tired of his purposeless lifestyle that left him feeling adrift. He realized he did not want to lose the love of Vanessa and that by committing to her, he could grow deeper roots and become more productive.

Robert was delighted to see the improvements in his after prints. He had developed numerous minor lines, denoting a conscious

ROBERT

Before

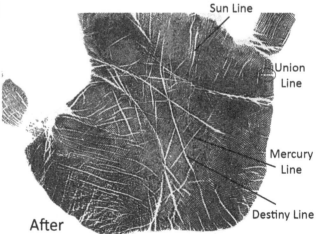

After

Fig. 8.4. Robert's before and after handprints

awareness of his abilities. Not only did his Destiny Line grow longer and stronger, denoting he found a purpose in life, he had developed a Sun Line, reflecting a more open heart and increased magnetism, as well as a Mercury Line, which allowed him to express himself more creatively. Perhaps the most encouraging minor line Robert developed is a Union Line, reflecting his dedication to Vanessa. In fact, he and Vanessa created a successful business together, had several children, and are still happily married decades later.

✦ HAPPINESS BLOCKER ✦

When the Destiny Line Stops at the Head Line

When our Destiny Line is blocked by the Head Line, it gets stuck in the middle of the hand and cannot ascend to the Mount of Saturn. Instead of our Head Line supporting and guiding our destiny, it becomes a line of obstruction; our thinking is getting in the way of fulfilling our purpose. This is a sign that our thoughts can be plagued with doubts, indecision, confusion, or lack of discernment.

So, while our mind can be a vehicle for expressing unimaginable possibilities through the Destiny Line, a blocked Destiny Line can limit our creative expression, especially if we use it to justify our poor choices. So, if our thoughts are tripping us up, we need to figure out how our way of thinking is sabotaging our happiness. When this is the case, we need to develop our powers of discernment so we can become

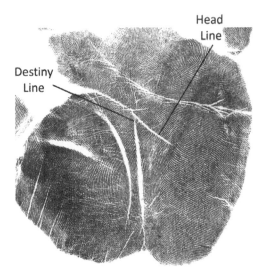

Fig. 8.5. The Destiny Line stopping at the Head Line

more objective and use our thoughts positively. In this way, we will find the motivation to push our Destiny Line past the Head Line to feel a renewed sense of inspiration.

When the Destiny Line Stops at the Heart Line

When the Destiny Line stops at the Heart Line, instead of our emotions motivating and encouraging us, they are quashing our inspiration and causing us to lose interest in pursuing our goal. When this is the case, we need to identify the source of our emotional turmoil and deal with it. For example, we can't allow heartache to interfere with our professional dreams or make emotional decisions that could derail our future prospects.

We need to increase our emotional intelligence so we can remain both passionate and objective.

Developing Our Destiny Line

The quickest way to develop a Destiny Line is by increasing our level of self-awareness. We must consciously comprehend who we are and what our purpose is in life. Both self-reflection and meditation are practices that will help develop and strengthen our Destiny Line. We can then embrace the fact that life is a blessing that provides us with the oppor-

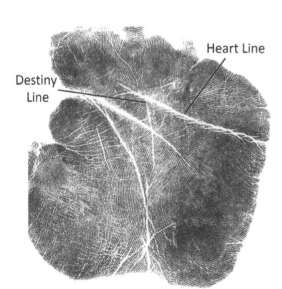

Heart Line

Destiny
Line

Fig. 8.6. The Destiny Line
stopping at the Heart Line

Fig. 8.7. Self-reflection and meditation help develop a strong Destiny Line.

tunity to discover our unique talents and express them to forge our special destiny.

✦ HAPPINESS BOOSTER ✦

Visualize a Longer, Stronger Destiny Line

We can fortify our purpose by visualizing the Destiny Line growing in depth, length, and strength. Envision a perfect Destiny Line in your palm, one that travels vertically without interruption from the base of the hand all the way to the Mount of Saturn. The more meaning and purpose we bring into our lives, the stronger our Destiny Line becomes.

Here Comes the Sun (Line)

Because the Destiny Line is charged with the discipline and endurance that come with Saturn's sense of responsibility, we don't want to feel overburdened by an arduous and demanding lifestyle. So let's celebrate life by embracing the passion, love, and joy that come with the development of the Sun Line. In the words of Maya Angelou: "My mission in life is not merely to survive, but to thrive; and to do so with some passion, some compassion, some humor, and some style."

So let's take a look at how to develop a Sun Line.

SUN LINE

Passion, Charisma, Success, and Joy

The Sun is the center of our solar system, and everything in our solar system revolves around it. This same energy is found in the Mount of Sun. It is the spark of universal light that illuminates us all.

Developing a Sun Line allows the best of our Sun mount to shine forth to the world. Our heart center opens and the barriers of ego fall to the wayside; it becomes easier for us to get in touch with our genuine self and be aware of the needs and concerns of others. This provides us with an irresistible charisma and magnetism that draw others to us. We can enjoy enormous success and happiness.

Portrait of the Sun Line

Ideally, a Sun Line appears on the Mount of Sun as a single, deep, vertical line that is free of any form of blockage or interference. We develop a Sun Line when our heart is totally engaged in something we are devoted to with all our passion.

By tapping into the immense potential of the Mount of Sun, the Sun Line allows us to channel its enormous creative energy to make even the most impossible dreams come true. The way to grow a Sun Line is by developing an abundance of self-confidence, dedication, and passion for life. Our passion radiates so powerfully that we exude an aura of charm, self-assurance, and joy. Consequently, harnessing our Sun energy attracts positive circumstances and people into our lives, further enhancing our happiness and success.

A Sun Line reveals that our heart is of singular purpose; it is not distracted or sidetracked by divergent or contradictory desires that pull us in different directions. This focused approach to life results in a steady heart—we remain constant in our thoughts, deeds, actions, and convictions regardless of the ups and downs we encounter in life. We pursue our goals with unwavering devotion and are not conflicted or

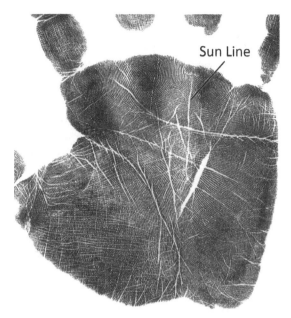

Sun Line

Fig. 8.8. The Sun Line

uncertain about who we are or what we are doing. Because there is no static in our mind, our heart shines through. Others are inspired by and drawn toward our warmth and sincerity; they sense there are no walls of ego separating us from them. We are able to touch their hearts because they feel our concern for their well-being is authentic. Consequently, we attract a large fan club of friends and supporters who are moved and inspired by our passionate zeal and dedication.

The moment we engage our heart by dedicating ourselves to a singular cause or pursuit that we passionately care about, we will ignite our Mount of Sun and a Sun Line will appear.

Let's find out what happens when the Sun Line is absent.

✦ HAPPINESS BLOCKER ✦
The Absent Sun Line

A faint or entirely absent Sun Line tells us we are not tapping into the infinite potential of our Sun energy or using its enormous creative power to make our wildest dreams come true. Indeed, we are not fully engaging our thoughts or feelings, hence we are not living life to the fullest. Either we have not defined what our heart is really longing for,

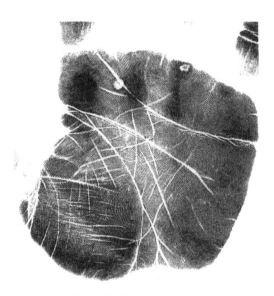

Fig. 8.9. Absent Sun Line

or, even if we have, we lack the faith or confidence that we are capable of achieving it.

Let's find out what we can do to develop a Sun Line.

✦ HAPPINESS BOOSTER ✦

Develop a Sun Line

To create and/or develop a strong Sun Line, we have to employ meditation and self-reflection in order to search within our heart and discover what it is that makes us feel truly alive and joyful. Then we must apply the mental focus and concentration to go for what we believe true happiness and success is—be it fame, excelling at sports, creating great art, reaching the top of our profession, or raising a healthy, loving family. Whatever it is, it is something that will fully engage our heart and that we will pursue with our entire being. Through our dedication, we will radiate joy and happiness, bringing warmth and inspiration to everyone in our life. In the end, we will not only have a Sun Line, but we will be satisfied and content with who we are and what we are doing.

◆◆◆

JULIETTE POWELL'S STORY
Igniting Her Sun Energy

Juliette Powell is a textbook case of how we can revitalize a weak Sun. She is the daughter of a French-Canadian mother and African American father, who parted ways with the family when Juliette was just a child.

Understandably, Juliette experienced an identity crisis growing up. She could not help but notice the difference between her own brown skin and her mother's white complexion.

At school, she was the only biracial student and the tallest kid in her class. Consequently, Juliette was self-conscious, shy, and lacking in confidence, all the way through her early teenage years. This is reflected in her before handprint. Her underactive Sun energy, denoting inhibition, is confirmed by her closed-in fingers.

Fig. 8.10. Juliette and Guylaine

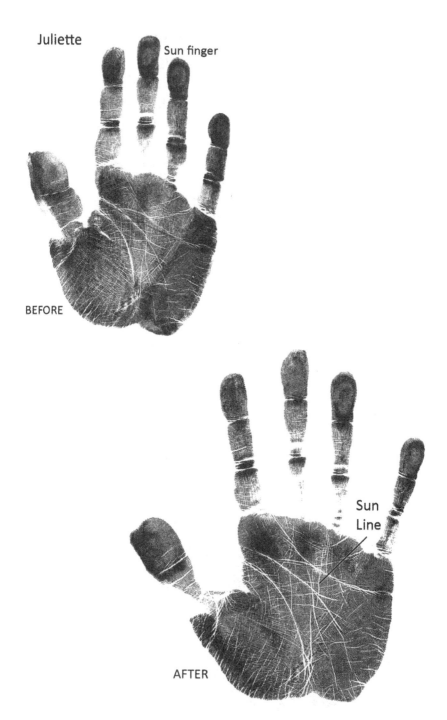

Fig. 8.11. Juliette's before and after handprints

Juliette had the support of her mother, who continually assured her that she was capable of doing anything she wanted to do in life and that she should never doubt herself. Although no person of color had ever won the Miss Canada national pageant, Juliette entered it on a dare and won. She later represented the country in the Miss Universe pageant. Juliette's good looks, smarts, and charismatic personality earned her a position as a veejay on MTV.

Her emerging Sun energy not only gave her confidence, it lit her way to success. She embraced the differences that once made her hide from the spotlight. In her after handprint, taken several years later, we see a strong Sun Line. Her fingers have fully opened, providing the space for her ring finger, the Sun finger, to breathe. Juliette began sharing her success story at local schools, hoping to inspire children to resist self-doubt and low self-esteem. With a little confidence and faith, they could reach the stars.

Islands in the Sun:
The Perils of Blocked Air

When our Air element is not flowing freely, it becomes stagnant. When this happens, we can feel congested and find it difficult to go with the flow physically, mentally, and socially.

A blocked Air element can manifest in the hand as an islanded Sun Line. The charisma that radiates from a free-flowing Air element is turned upside down when our Air is blocked. Instead of having a fan club, we attract criticism.

When we are in this situation, we have to turn our magnetism around—so instead of repelling people we can attract them. To do this requires a little soul searching. We must ask ourselves why we are attracting negativity into our life instead of being loved and appreciated. Then, we must ensure that our words and actions are so genuine and caring that no one can doubt our good intentions. In that case, even if we receive criticism, because we are confident in our heart that our motives are pure, we remain unaffected, and the island in our Sun Line will disappear. As Paramahansa Yogananda says: "There is a magnet in your heart that will attract true friends. That magnet is unselfishness, thinking of others first; when you learn to live for others, they will live for you."

Fig. 8.12. Islanded Sun Line

An excellent tool for improving our Air element is, you guessed it, pranayama. Indeed, proper breathing can enliven our Air element and bring a sparkle back to our eyes in just a matter of weeks.

✦ HAPPINESS BOOSTER ✦

Be Happy in Others' Happiness

A Sun Line is produced by the power of the love and passion we experience when we care for something very deeply—it is a power that connects us directly to our heart, which in turn ignites our personal magnetism as people feel our authenticity.

It takes a great amount of soul-searching to get in touch with the depth of our heart because our mind keeps us distracted and preoccupied with so many concerns. Disconnected from our heart it is difficult to be happy, not to mention be mindful of the needs of others.

Fig. 8.13. Grow a Sun Line: We are all facets of one living whole,
so be happy in others' happiness.

Fortunately, the secret for growing a Sun Line was handed
down to us by Ghanshyam's grandfather who said to "always be
happy in others' happiness." How do we do this? By first seeking our own happiness from within so that our heart is so filled
with love, we have no choice but to rejoice in the happiness and
success of everyone in our lives. In this way, the megawatt brilliance of our Sun energy will be fully ignited.

However, to get the most out of our Sun Line, we must go
beyond the limited element of Air and connect with the expansive
element of Ether, which, as we know, is associated with the Mount
of Mercury.

MERCURY LINE

Transcending Our Way to Happiness

The Mercury Line is one of the most auspicious lines in palmistry, and it's one that we most certainly want to develop. Why? Because it tells us that we are bringing out the very best of our Mercury energy. This mystical line reveals our ability to convey our thoughts, feelings, concepts, and ideas with ease and eloquence. We are boosted by a sense of joy because our connection to the ether enables us to recognize our infinite nature.

The Mercury Line ideally originates from the Life Line and travels diagonally past the lines of Head and Heart to terminate on the Mount of Mercury unbroken and without interferences.

It is the Line of Transcendence because it connects the world of matter, including our physical self (the Mount of Venus), with the world of Spirit and our higher self (the Mount of Mercury). This nonphysical aspect of who we are is regarded by the sages as our true self as it is infinite and survives beyond our physical death. With a Mercury Line we have the ability to bypass the constraints of limited thinking and avoid the emotional turmoil of personal dramas. Indeed, the Mercury Line connects us to the most discerning aspect of our mind, Budh.

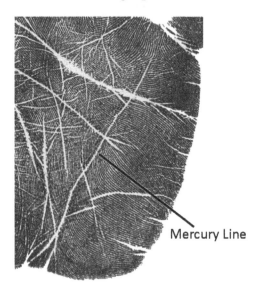

Mercury Line

Fig. 8.14. The Mercury Line

Making Budh Your Buddy

In Sanskrit, Mercury is known as *Budh*, a wide-ranging term that refers to the awakened mind and can variously mean knowing, awareness, understanding, comprehension, communicating, and imparting wisdom. Indeed, this is why the Buddha, whose name derives from this root word, is known as "The Enlightened One."

The Mercury Line, like Buddha, encourages us to search for the true joy in life. The Buddha discovered that peace and happiness could be found by going inward and realizing that everything external was finite and impermanent. This is why Buddha, who was born a prince, was motivated to abandon all material attachments in his pursuit of truth and lasting happiness.

Happiness beyond Attachment

The presence of the Mercury Line is our assurance that, like Buddha, we are not attached to the fruits of our action; we live in the moment,

Fig. 8.15. The peace and contentment
of the Buddha

free of expectation. For example, if we are booed after giving a speech, it does not affect us. Because our heart and mind are fixed on sharing our message, we are not attached to applause and are therefore able to keep our sense of humor. Our only expectation is that we are doing our best, totally engaged. We are not looking for outside praise because the work we do is reward enough; we find satisfaction and joy simply by having the opportunity to use our gifts and talents creatively.

Living Fully in the Present

With a Mercury Line we can never be bored; we are completely focused and fully engaged in the present moment, aware and attentive. Because we are totally involved in what we are doing, we rise above the constraints of time and space. For example, absorbed in teaching her class, a professor doesn't realize that two hours have gone by. It truly feels like a second! Likewise, hours fly by like minutes for the child at the zoo, while for his guardian, who would rather be golfing, it seems like an eternity.

However, when we do something that has little meaning for us—for example, doing our tax returns when we would prefer to be at the movies with our friends—our heart and mind are not really engaged. Time

Fig. 8.16. Being fully engaged in the present moment

seems to drag on endlessly. When this is the case, our Mercury Line is missing, broken, or interfered with.

A strong Mercury Line can make us forget that we are hungry or tired, or even that we are in pain. For example, a professional skater may take a prize for her breathtaking performance unaware that her ankle is broken.

When we have a Mercury Line, we can make even the toughest of projects look easy—what may take hours for another person to do, we can finish in a flash. As the Line of Transcendence, it keeps us from getting bogged down by life and the environment around us. The scientist can work for ten hours solid to come up with his cure. Physical needs, mental preoccupations, emotional upheavals—nothing can distract us from our focused, joyful self-expression.

Mercury as the Line of Communication

The Mercury Line relates to the god Mercury, or Hermes, the winged messenger of the gods. Having a Mercury Line enables us to tap into the world of ideas and inventions for the betterment of humanity. Not only do we have the gift of gab, but we are able to listen to what people are saying to us without being distracted in our mind or emotions by what's going on around us. Indeed, the Mercury Line is found on the hands of great storytellers who can use their powers of communication to make us forget ourselves. We sit rapt with attention as they carry us on a trip that makes two hours seem like the blink of an eye!

Mercury, Ether, and the Throat Chakra

By developing a Mercury Line we ignite our Mount of Mercury, element of Ether, and throat chakra; we are becoming fully engaged in life and enjoying every minute of it. Because we are connecting to the Ether element—the Akash—we recognize that we are all part of the universal family connected through Spirit. Hence, we feel comfortable and at home no matter where we are; our sense of humor and open nature put everyone around us at ease.

And because Mercury is able to peer through the portal of infinity and recognize the eternal joy that is Spirit, the presence of a Mercury Line can then impart that beautiful vision to us, putting our problems into perspective. Indeed, when we experience even a moment of that

Fig. 8.17. Mercury: Peering through the portal to infinity

joy, we become detached from the grip our hurts, disappointments, and thwarted expectations have on us.

The good news is that we all have the ability to develop a Mercury Line and connect with the Akash through Mercury.

✦ HAPPINESS BOOSTER ✦

Cut the Static with a Mercury Line

With a Mercury line our consciousness is like a cosmic radio—there is so little static in our mind that we can tune in to the Akash without any interference. This makes us highly intuitive, allowing us to be at the right place at the right time for the right success.

We see this attunement to our inner Akash in the "Great One," former NHL superstar Wayne Gretzky, who wowed fans for decades with his uncanny ability to anticipate where the puck would be at any given moment and sense the moves the players around him would make in advance. Like a master chess player, he

Fig. 8.18. The Great One: Wayne Gretzky

possessed the skill, presence of mind, and intuitive powers to see the outcome of a game before it was played, allowing him to score goals before anyone had a chance to see him coming.

✦ **HAPPINESS BLOCKER** ✦

Absent Mercury Line

An absence of a Mercury Line shows we are not activating our Mount of Mercury and our inner Hermes, the messenger of the gods, capable of moving freely between the worlds of the mortal and divine. We are missing the bridge that connects matter with our consciousness, hence we are not utilizing our Akash. We are not attuned with space—neither with the vastness of our inner space, where our mind can travel into the

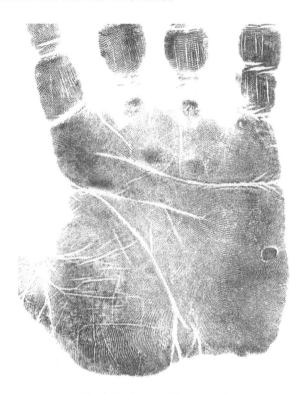

Fig. 8.19. Absent Mercury Line

world of ideas and invention, nor with the outer space of our environment, which includes the people and events that surround us. We may be oblivious to what others are trying to communicate to us through words, body language, or attitude.

Instead of an ease of expression, there is an exertion of energy taking place as we try to express ourselves and get our ideas across.

So how do we grow a Mercury Line? Let's find out.

✦ HAPPINESS BOOSTER ✦

Grow a Mercury Line

To develop a Mercury Line we must develop our powers of concentration to such a degree that we can keep our mind focused on our goal without being distracted, forgetful, or inattentive. We must shut out background noise so we can tune in to our inner voice. It is in the silence of reflective meditation that we find true

Fig. 8.20. Listening to others with an attentive mind and
open heart helps to grow a Mercury Line.

guidance and learn to hone our power of intuition, which are the
tools of effortless self-expression and communication.

Developing the fine art of listening to what others are *really*
communicating to us gives us the gift of walking in another person's shoes. It is through that experience that we develop the
qualities of empathy and compassion. As we refine this skill, we
will not only get along with others better and be able to talk to
them more openly and freely, but we will be able to intuit how
they are feeling and know exactly what we need to do or say to
comfort them. In short, the fastest route to develop a Mercury
Line requires us to listen to others with an attentive mind and
open heart, speak kindly to everyone, and maintain our sense
of humor.

Not only do we need to develop a Mercury Line, we need to nurture it. If we don't, we could lose it. It's a lesson Patrice learned the
hard way.

---------◆◆◆---------

PATRICE'S STORY
Lost Voice: The Need to Nurture Our Mercury Line

The law of conservation states that energy can neither be created nor destroyed; it just changes form. We see this in the case of Patrice, whose very first set of handprints revealed an incredibly well-developed Mercury Line. Indeed, Patrice was immersed in the Akash, which he manifested through his writing and poetry. However, when his after prints were taken a year later, his magnificent Mercury Line has all but disappeared. What could have happened that caused him to lose his access to the Akash?

It turns out that Patrice had to put his writing aside for a year to help out with the family business. Unfortunately, he was forced to work with a relative who was a bully, which made Patrice constantly fearful, nervous, and anxious. Those negative thoughts and emotions literally dissolved his Mercury Line. Indeed, at his follow-up consultation, Patrice was a shadow of his former self; he had lost the desire to write or express himself through the beautiful words of his poetry.

Fortunately, Patrice realized the profound effect thoughts have on us, either good or bad. He understood that it was his thoughts that created his Mercury Line and it was his thoughts that made it disappear. In other words, he acknowledged the law of conservation and was determined to use positive thinking to restore his Mercury Line and reengage his passion for writing.

---------◆◆◆---------

IVAN'S STORY
Finding His Voice: A Mercury Miracle

Ivan's first handprint was taken when he was attending college. At that time he was confused and lacked direction. Nevertheless, he engaged his heart and mind through his studies and completed his PhD in comparative religion. Indeed, Ivan eventually became a professor of philosophy and was loved by all his students. Ivan's ability to tap into his Mercury energy and express himself effortlessly is confirmed in his after handprint by the presence of a Mercury Line. (See Ivan's handprints in fig. 8.22 on page 196.)

PATRICE

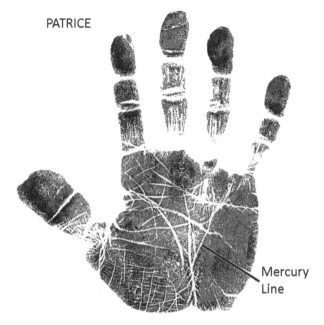

Mercury
Line

BEFORE

AFTER

Fig. 8.21. Patrice's before and after handprints

IVAN

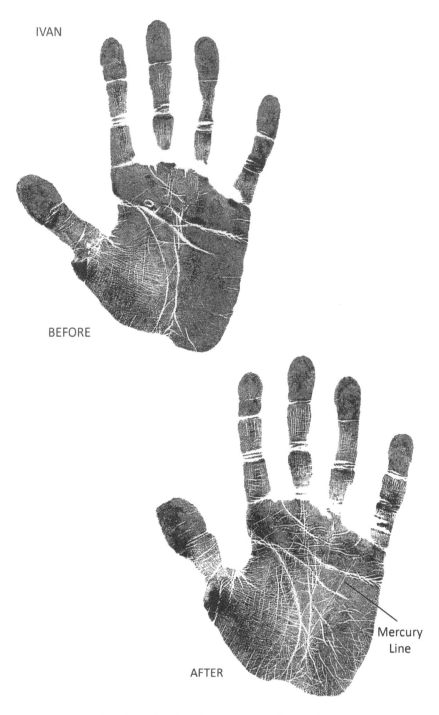

BEFORE

AFTER

Mercury
Line

Fig. 8.22. Ivan's before and after handprints

GIRDLE OF VENUS

A Permanent Smile Stamped on Our Heart

A Girdle of Venus appears in the upper section of the hand as a fully formed semicircle resembling a smile. With its close proximity to the Heart Line, the ideally formed Girdle of Venus reflects our capacity to love, feel deeply, and be moved by the goodness and beauty we see and experience in the world around us. Our heightened sensitivity allows us to transmute our emotions into a creative expression that touches and moves the hearts of others. Hence, it should come as no surprise that Eastern texts describe the Girdle of Venus as one of the most auspicious signs in palmistry.

The positive, loving energy vibrating within a Girdle of Venus is so potent it is difficult to contain; we have a strong desire to use our particular gifts, skills, and talents to express and share all the love, beauty, and harmony we feel within us. We may do this through art, music, or drama; or as a healer, mentor, teacher, community leader, or philanthropist; or simply by building caring and supportive relationships with friends and family. Regardless of the medium we choose to express our inner joy, our words and actions will uplift and inspire others. A Girdle of Venus makes us artists of love and beauty—the world is our canvas.

Ideally travelling from Jupiter to Mercury without any breaks, the Girdle of Venus unites the five-fingered mounts and hence reflects a blossoming of the finest qualities within our elements and chakras, making it a major happiness booster.

Fig. 8.23. A Girdle of Venus

◆◆◆

SISTER MARGARET'S STORY

Spreading Love, Peace, and Happiness in a Troubled World

When World War II broke out, Sister Margaret was a young Catholic nun working in rural Japan. She was arrested by Japanese soldiers and spent four years in a brutal internment camp. She suffered great deprivation and witnessed many atrocities, but she never allowed her heart to be hardened by bitterness or hatred. After the war, she stayed on in Japan to care for orphans, treat the wounded, and help rebuild the country. Before returning to North America, she spent years traveling throughout Asia bringing aid and comfort to the poorest of the poor.

Sister Margaret invited former Japanese soldiers—her onetime enemies and captors—to attend one of her peace conferences, and she embraced each and every one of them with kindness and warmth. She explained her reason for it: "We all struggle with darkness, but we are also all children of God, touched by Divine light. It is our job to let that light shine from us and help it shine in others. If we make that our mission in life, we'll all be better people, and this world will be a much better place."

From her prints, you can see Sister Margaret has a beautiful Girdle of Venus hovering above her Heart Line. Sister Margaret lived into her

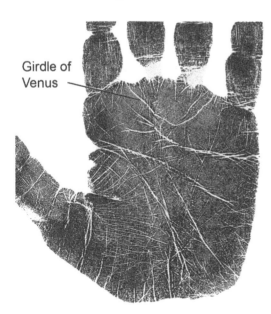

Girdle of
Venus

Fig. 8.24. Sister Margaret's
Girdle of Venus

nineties and never stopped working to create international and interpersonal peace, harmony, understanding, and forgiveness. Her handprint, with its remarkable Girdle of Venus, is a lasting testament to a beautiful life, well lived.

✦ **HAPPINESS BLOCKER** ✦

The Fragmented Girdle

As the Girdle of Venus is located in the area of the Heart Line, too many scattered lines can scramble our emotions and interfere with the smooth flow of the heart. When there are too many disjointed lines crossing the four upper mounts, it creates static on each of the mounts. This results in emotional commotion preventing a clear channel for us to express our feelings harmoniously. Consequently, rather than acting to stimulate the creative process in a constructive way, we can easily be lost in overemotionalism and excessive sentimentality, making us moody, subjective, and compulsive. We may even try to avoid our pain by escaping reality through drugs, alcohol, promiscuity, or a fantasy world of our own creation.

However, despite the anxiety and tumultuous emotional state it may produce, having a broken Girdle of Venus is still preferable to having no girdle at all. The presence of any girdle awakens our feeling nature; it opens our heart and sensitizes us to life, to our own feelings, and to the feelings of others.

Fig. 8.25. A fragmented Girdle of Venus

Mending a Broken Girdle of Venus

To restore balance to a fragmented Girdle of Venus, we must realize that our profound sensitivity is a gift that is capable of lifting us out of the ordinary and mundane to experience peaks of bliss, love, fulfillment, and a sense of meaningfulness. If we can find a creative outlet into which to channel our sensitivity, we can inspire others and more fully enjoy our relationships and life in general.

Now to do this is a mighty task, for how do you control a highly emotional nature? We have to be willing to discipline ourselves and pour our heart completely into a creative avenue without trying to escape when our feelings are hurt or challenges arise. We must not be daunted by our failures and carry on, trying to perfect the expression of our sensitivity through whatever creative gifts or talents we possess. In order to do that, we must be willing to put our pride aside and accept the critique of others with good humor.

----------◆◆◆----------

GARY'S STORY
We Can All Have a Smile in Our Heart

While the Mount of Venus reflects a physical appreciation and expression of love, the Girdle of Venus is more sublime and universal in scope. Hence, to develop a girdle, we must melt any resistance coating our heart in order to heighten our sensory awareness, be sensitive to the beauty of existence, and express that beauty through the noblest of human qualities, such as appreciation, consideration, kindness, gratitude, and unconditional love. We do this when we stop seeing ourselves as isolated and separate from others and recognize we are connected to all living souls. We must become aware of the need to love our neighbors as well as ourselves. This is not necessarily an esoteric pursuit; it's a goal anyone can achieve through simple and practical choices—as we see in the case of Gary.

At the time of his first handprint, Gary was going through a contentious divorce that was draining him physically and emotionally. Fortunately, he recognized that part of the reason for his failed relationship was his inability to express himself freely and openly.

To his credit, Gary decided to leave his anguish and heartache

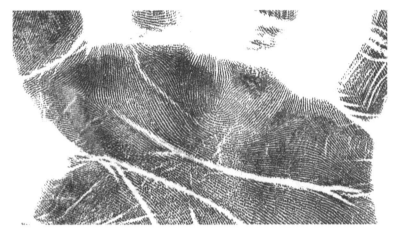

BEFORE

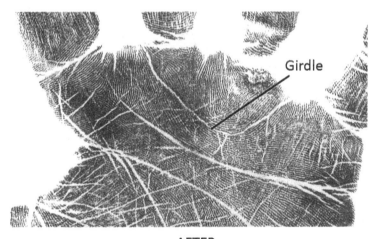

Girdle

AFTER

Fig. 8.26. Gary's before and after handprints

behind and focus on a brighter and happier future. He began group therapy, returned to school, and tried to maintain a positive outlook on life. Eventually he became a therapist and attracted a devoted following of clients who were drawn by his empathy. Thanks to this, his after handprint has a Girdle of Venus, revealing that his heart has melted; his heightened sensitivity has opened him to the beauty of life, bringing him a sense of joy that he naturally radiates to others.

Signs of Happiness and How to Grow Them

If you have been following along, you'll know by now that when the energies of our hand are in harmony, there will be happiness in our lives. That joy is reflected in our palm when the mounts begin to display the signs of happiness, which include markings such as a star on Sun, healing stigmata on Mercury, or a grille on Venus.

These auspicious signs blossom as we grow in wisdom and gain momentum in our pursuit of a more joyful existence, personal fulfillment, and spiritual growth. Often referred to as wisdom markings, these signs of happiness manifest when we are expressing the finest qualities of a mount.

Let's begin our exploration of these magnificent markings with the grille on Venus.

THE GRILLE ON VENUS
Love in Action

As we know, Venus is the mount of love and reflects our capacity to love deeply. The appearance of a symmetrical grille on Venus—one composed of an equal number of vertical and horizontal lines—is a very auspicious sign (see fig. 9.2 on page 204). It has been poetically described as nature's stamp of approval on Venus, which means we possess a warmth and charisma others find irresistible; we attract love like bees to honey.

1. Grill on Venus
2. Star on Jupiter
3. Cross on Jupiter
4. Love of Truth Line
5. Star on Sun
6. Healing Stigmata
7. Union Line

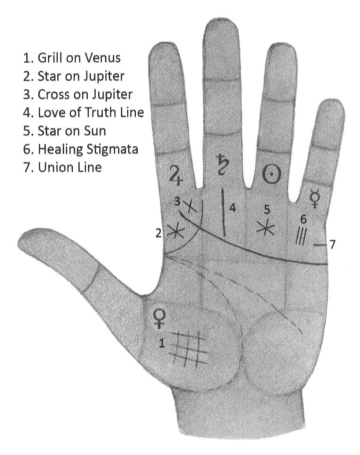

Fig. 9.1. Signs of happiness

A grille reflects a heartfelt urge to connect with others and openly share our feelings of love with them. It denotes a sincere and caring nature as well as a concern for the well-being of the people in our lives. We delight in the sense-related pleasures that Venus has to offer; possess a desire to communicate with warmth, comfort, and joy; and strive to create beauty and harmony in all our relationships and endeavors. The grille makes us very likeable; others sense the depth and authenticity of our feelings and respond appreciatively.

A grille on Venus not only makes us gracious, genial, and a joy to be around, it boosts our magnetism and draws admiration for our creative Venus energy and ingenuity.

We see this in the case of Edward.

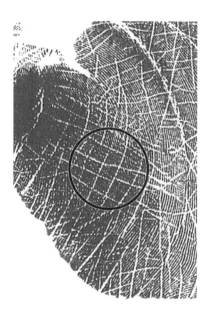

Fig. 9.2. The symmetrical grille on Venus

◆◆◆

EDWARD'S STORY

Mr. Nice Guy

Edward has a beautifully formed grille, which shows he is expressing heartfelt, constructive, and affectionate feelings in all his interpersonal relationships. His serene, positive energy brings calmness to his workplace, and he inspires passion in his colleagues through his creativity

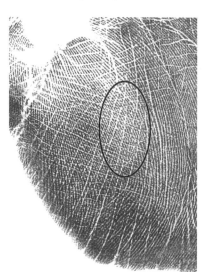

Fig. 9.3. Edward's symmetrical grille

and innovative ideas. Everybody loves him, and he is described by any-one who has spent time with him as an all-round nice guy.

✦ HAPPINESS BOOSTER ✦

Developing a Grille on Venus

To develop a symmetrical grille, we first need to develop vertical lines on the Mount of Venus, which we do by diving deeply into our loving nature. Secondly, we must develop the horizontal lines by expressing that love in all we say and do. By doing this, we imbue our love with a spiritual dimension that looks beyond our own concerns and comfort to extend care and nurturance to the people in our lives. Indeed, fueling our love with selflessness and compassion for everyone makes us a force of love in the world.

Additionally, and as we have learned, Venus is a reflection of our physical self, so by taking care of our body, we are taking care of the element of Earth and first (coccyx) chakra. This pro-vides us with a strong foundation that gives us a sense of per-sonal safety and security, allowing our life force prana to ascend the spine and ignite the energy within all the other elements and chakras. Developing the qualities of dependability, reliability, and conscientiousness within ourselves goes a long way in solidifying our foundation.

✦ HAPPINESS BLOCKER ✦

A Nonsymmetrical Grille on Venus

Problems will arise when a grille on Venus is nonsymmetrical—that is, when there is an imbalance between the number of vertical lines and the number of horizontal lines.

Having more vertical than horizontal lines tells us that although our love is deep, we are hesitant to express it. To correct this, we need to be less reserved in the expression of our care and affection.

Having more horizontal than vertical lines can propel us to extend ourselves to the point of exhaustion. To address this, we must make sure we take the time to refuel our energy reserves so we can continue to love and support others.

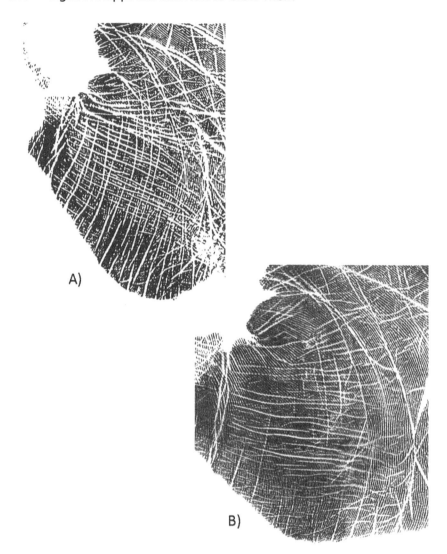

Fig. 9.4. (A) More vertical than horizontal lines;
(B) More horizontal than vertical lines

THREE SIGNS OF HAPPINESS
ON JUPITER

Ring of Solomon, Cross, and Star

As we have learned, our thoughts and actions can lead to specific
changes in our palm. On our Mount of Jupiter, the mount related to

finding our individual purpose, we have the ability to develop a Ring of Solomon, a cross, and/or a star when our ambition to succeed also embraces the prosperity and joy of others.

The Ring of Solomon

A Love of Humanity

Named after King Solomon, reputedly the wisest person who ever lived, a Ring of Solomon, forming a semicircle around the Mount of Jupiter, is a sign of wisdom reflecting our ability to understand, relate to, and empathize with other people. We have a profound understanding of human nature and are extremely sensitive to the feelings and problems of others. With a ring, we are philanthropic and naturally gravitate toward the helping and healing professions, including all forms of counseling.

The Ring of Solomon indicates our ego and ambition have been baptized with wisdom, empathy, and humility. Our ego is no longer running wild; it is restrained, deepened, and perfected within the boundary of the ring's semicircle.

In Vedic culture, a Ring of Solomon is referred to as *Guru Diksha Rekha*, denoting a deep desire to connect with a mentor who can guide us toward spiritual wisdom.

Fig. 9.5. Ring of Solomon

Ring of
Solomon

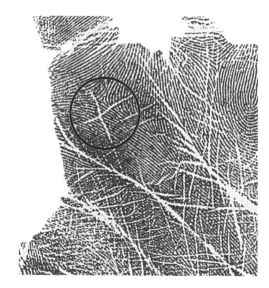

Fig. 9.6. Cross on Jupiter

The Cross

Fulfilling Our Purpose with a Little Help from Our Friends

A cross on Jupiter signals that we passionately want to discover our purpose in life. The four points of the cross symbolize that our desire to find meaning is so powerful that it is radiating to the four corners of the world. Our magnetism attracts the exact people with the specific skills, talents, and temperament needed to help us realize our dreams and fulfill our destiny in a way that contributes to the betterment of humanity.

The Star

Enjoying Outstanding Success in All Our Pursuits

A star on Jupiter shows we have developed a level of skill and expertise that has earned us recognition and fame. It indicates that we can have outstanding success in any area that we focus our ambition—social, material, intellectual, or spiritual. It is said that the star on Jupiter denotes our ability to perceive through our third eye, which is often described as the "Gateway to the Eternal." Indeed, we can actually see a star when we are in deep meditation, giving us a feeling of profound connection to all humankind: the ultimate expansion of Jupiter. We understand we are not separate beings and celebrate the success of others as our own.

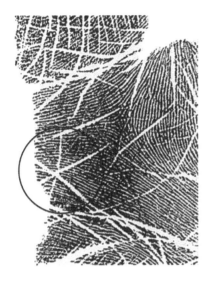

Fig. 9.7. Star on Jupiter

✦ HAPPINESS BOOSTER ✦

Bringing Out the Best of Our Jupiter

Jupiter, as we know, is the mount of personal ambition as we strive to find our purpose in life, and we will develop a Ring of Solomon, a cross, and/or a star when our ambition to succeed includes the welfare and happiness of others. The fastest way to achieve this is to ensure our Jupiter-related Water element and second (sacral) chakra are balanced. We do this by developing Jupiter's best qualities, which are respect and consideration toward others, kindness, gentleness, and magnanimity.

DOUBLE HAPPINESS ON SATURN
The Love of Truth Line and the Trident

Our Mount of Saturn provides the opportunity for us to develop many positive signs, including the Love of Truth Line and the trident.

The Truth Line
Honest-to-Goodness Happiness

The Love of Truth is a vertical line found on the Mount of Saturn; it is an auspicious sign of wisdom that springs from a deep desire to find

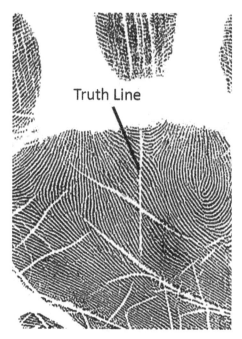

Fig. 9.8. Love of Truth Line on Saturn

the true meaning of life. We develop a Truth Line when we learn to use Saturn's painful experiences to become a wiser and more authentic version of ourselves.

Through self-reflection, we transform the anguish of our thwarted desires and dashed expectations into self-awareness, wisdom, and compassion. Our desire to understand our true nature is often so strong it sets us on a spiritual quest, which is why the Love of Truth Line is often referred to as the Love of God Line.

The Trident

Sharing Our Wisdom with Others

A trident on the Mount of Saturn shows we have emerged victorious from the fires of Saturn having turned our gyana into guna. As we learned in chapter 7, that means we have successfully transformed the knowledge gained through painful experiences into wisdom and virtue, qualities that now guide our lives. Our insight into the human condition gives us the ability to bring happiness to others by teaching divine sciences and imparting metaphysical truths.

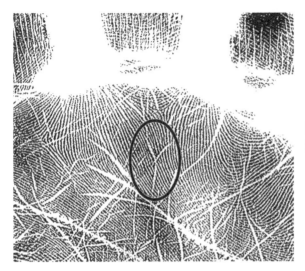

Fig. 9.9. Trident on
Saturn

✦ HAPPINESS BOOSTER ✦

Grow Wisdom Signs on Saturn

As we've learned, Saturn is the stern teacher whose harsh life lessons force our consciousness to transform and evolve. Saturn's Fire element, related to the third (lumbar) chakra, aids in this "smelting process" by converting the raw ore of our nature into pure gold. But we must play our part, first by being receptive to constructive criticism, advice, and guidance. We then must develop the qualities of fortitude, discipline, and a willingness to sit in quiet reflection or meditation to discover our true self and the true meaning of existence. In this way, the transformative flames of Saturn melt away the dross of ego resistance to reveal a genuine, pure, and happy heart.

THREE HAPPINESS BLOCKERS
ON SATURN

A Grille, Ring, or Star

It is no surprise that less auspicious signs can also appear on our Mount of Saturn: A grille, ring, or star. However, these signs also provide us with opportunities for personal growth.

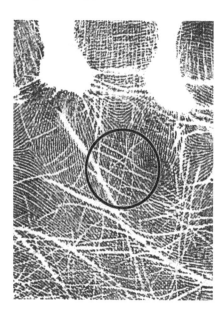

Fig. 9.10. A grille on Saturn

The Grille

Difficulty Processing Our Thoughts and Our Food

While a grille on Venus is auspicious, a grille on Saturn is a mixed bag of energies. It is a combination of positive vertical lines and negative horizontal lines. The vertical lines show that we are aspiring to find the truth; the horizontal lines denote obstacles blocking our way. Hence, the grille denotes a constant sense of tension and frustration.

Psychologically, a grille denotes we are struggling to process something that is bothering us—such as an unkind remark, unfair treatment, or criticism that could be either warranted or unfounded. On a physical level, the grille could indicate problems with our digestion.

The Ring of Saturn

Trapped in Our Own Thoughts

The Ring of Saturn forms a semicircle on the mount and denotes we are stuck in our Saturn energy. Instead of using the Fire element to transform our difficult life experiences into life lessons, we ruminate over past hurts and grievances, unable to let them go. This can lead to negative thinking and a melancholy nature that traps us in our mind and isolates us from others. We might not even be aware we are emotionally freezing out the people in our lives.

Ring of Saturn

Fig. 9.11. Ring of Saturn

The Star

Holding On to Grievances

A star on Saturn intensifies the bitterness we feel when witnessing injustices being done around us or to us. We have a tendency to hold on to the anguish and anger that these injustices inflame within us. And, due to the universal law of attraction, we can draw angry people into our lives. To mitigate the influence of a Saturnian star, we must adopt

Fig. 9.12. A star on Saturn

one of Saturn's many mottos: "Forgive, forget, and move on." However, if we fail to let go of our grievances, the accumulated energy of our resentment, denoted by a star, can negatively impact our life. We see this in the case of Noa.

◆◆◆

NOA'S STORY
A Refugee Struggling to Let Go of the Past

Noa is having difficulty letting go of painful childhood memories, which is confirmed by the presence of the prominent star we see on her Mount of Saturn. When she was a young teen, she was awakened in the middle of the night by the sound of nearby gunfire and explosions. Covered in dust, she quickly gathered a few things and rushed outside only to discover bodies scattered outside her family home. A neighbor grabbed her and took her to a shelter where she spent several terrifying months.

Noa endured many indignities and remembers people viciously fighting over scraps of food or a mouthful of clean water. She blamed the insurgents for the pain and suffering she went through and for destroying the peace she had known her entire life. Even many years later, she was still unable to forget the miseries she had experienced.

Until she learns to heal her heart by letting go of her hurt and suffering, her present life will continue to be impacted by her past. To dissolve

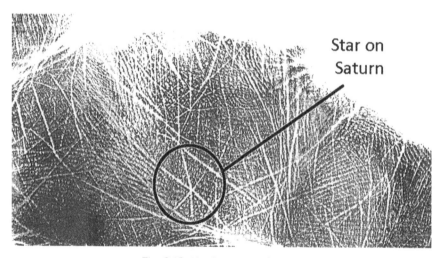

Star on Saturn

Fig. 9.13. Noa's star on Saturn

her star on Saturn, find solace, and bring joy to herself and her family, she must look inward and connect to the loving impulses of her heart.

Don't fret if you find a star or a couple of other negative markings on your Saturn. By developing a Truth Line (which we learned to do on pages 209–10), we can disperse any negativity from our Saturn mount. However, growing a Truth Line requires us to accept Saturn's painful experiences and, like an alchemist, transmute them into wisdom, forgiveness, and compassion.

✦ HAPPINESS BOOSTER ✦

How to Eliminate a Saturnian Grille, Ring, or Star

The quickest way to eliminate a grille, ring, or star on Saturn is by growing a Love of Truth Line. That's because a Love of Truth Line acts as a channel through which we can positively direct Saturnian energy rather than allowing it to build up inside of us and turn us bitter. But how do we do this? By letting go of our grievances and using the painful life lessons of Saturn to become more loving, wise, and compassionate. Otherwise, Saturn will become a malefic force in our life and block us from accessing the joyful energy of its neighboring Sun mount and heart chakra.

RADIANT LOVE ON THE MOUNT OF SUN

Harnessing the Megawatt Brilliance
of the Sun

A star on the Mount of Sun is like a supernova explosion of love in our hand. It's a sign that tells us the megawatt brilliance of our Sun energy has been fully ignited. Our dedication to pursuing our dreams and passions has carried us through the trials and tribulations of Saturn to open wide the doors of our heart, allowing our true self to shine through. Our authentic nature is hard to resist, and we radiate with a powerful charisma that makes us magnets of love; people want to be in our company because they feel inspired and uplifted.

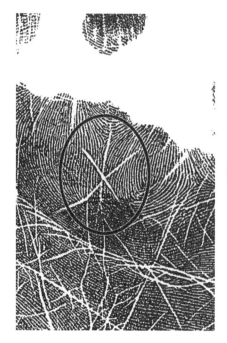

Fig. 9.14. A star on Sun

✦ HAPPINESS BOOSTER ✦

A Star Is Born

We can all tap into the inner brilliance of our Sun energy and create a star simply by being our authentic self and being passionate in whatever we do. This will connect us with our heart chakra and infuse our being with boundless love and joy, and, thanks to the element of Air, those warm feelings will be shared with all. Developing the heart chakra requires sincerity. We must strip all pretense from the way in which we express our emotions. In other words, we must convey our feelings, particularly our feelings of love, without expectation and in the most genuine and authentic manner possible. In this way, a star is born.

However, the Mount of Sun is also a place where negative signs can appear, such as a grille—a major happiness blocker—at least until we recognize it and make changes accordingly.

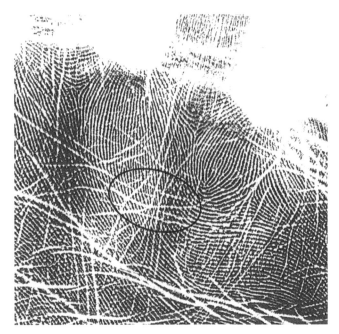

Fig. 9.15. A grille on Sun

A Grille on Sun

A grille on the Mount of Sun is made up of a combination of vertical lines, which reflect our desire to succeed, and horizontal lines, which denote we are encountering many obstacles blocking our path. The result could be a great deal of frustration. To rid ourselves of the troublesome horizontal lines requires us to step back and examine situations that we find frustrating in a more objective light. This will teach us what we need to learn to surmount any obstacles blocking our Sun energy. By staying focused and committed, the horizontal lines will fade, leaving us only with an auspicious, solid, singular line of Sun.

POWERFUL SIGNS OF HAPPINESS ON MERCURY

The Healing Stigmata and Union Line

As the mount of communication and enlightenment, Mercury is the home of two auspicious signs that tell us we are bringing happiness and healing to the people in our life: the healing stigmata and the Union Line. Let's explore the meaning of these signs and how to develop them.

The Healing Stigmata

Mercury is a magnificent mount that bestows upon us many mystical gifts, including the gift of healing. When our care and concern for others grow deep and profound, we will develop three parallel diagonal lines on the mount known as the "healing stigmata." A stigmata reflects the joy we experience when we extend comfort to others, be it physical, emotional, mental, or spiritual. We are tuned in to Mercury's intuitive Ether element, which blesses us with the insight of knowing exactly what to say and do to alleviate suffering and bring joy. Indeed, we are natural healers, so it should come as no surprise that a healing stigmata is often found on the hands of those in the healing professions.

✦ HAPPINESS BOOSTER ✦

Growing a Healing Stigmata

The more we care for others, the quicker our healing stigmata will grow, whether it is a kind word for someone who is feeling low, a

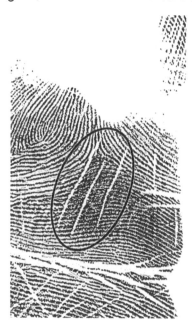

Fig. 9.16. A healing stigmata on Mercury

pat on the back, bringing a cup of tea, or a motivational talk that inspires thousands on a YouTube channel. Developing our intuition and empathy will help attune us to the needs of others; it will also help us to be good listeners and use our natural talent for healing to console and comfort—all of which promote the growth of a stigmata.

However, one of the biggest challenges in growing a stigmata is getting trapped in the endless 24/7 bombardment of news, information, and entertainment that is virtually inescapable in the twenty-first century. All that mental static makes it difficult for us to connect to the Ether and to attune to the needs of others. Hence, to increase our intuition and grow a stigmata, we must set aside time for quiet meditation and reflection as often as we can, hopefully every day.

A Union Line

The Line of Commitment

The Union Line, also known as the Marriage or Relationship Line, denotes a willingness to make a commitment to another and put down roots. It is highly karmic in nature, denoting that, from the billions of

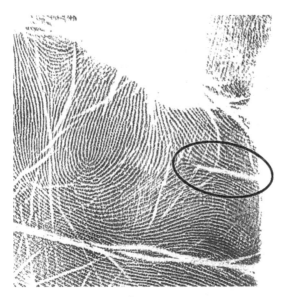

Fig. 9.17. A Union Line on Mercury

people on the planet, we have been drawn to that special partnership the universe has designed for us to enjoy, learn from, and grow as an individual. This applies to any relationship that we fully commit our heart to—be it passionate or platonic, spiritual or worldly.

It may seem incongruous that the line reflecting our deepest level of attachment appears on Mercury, the mount of detachment, but it's not incongruous at all. Why? Because Mercury, as the mount of enlightenment, teaches us to transform attachment into commitment and devotion. The presence of a Union Line provides us with the opportunity to open our heart and place another's happiness before our own.

✦ HAPPINESS BLOCKER ✦
Multiple Union Lines and the Emptiness
of the Hungry Heart

Multiple Union Lines denote fleeting interests that take us from one person to another without giving any serious thought to maintaining a single-hearted, single-minded relationship. We are not fulfilling our karmic debts but creating karma by leaving a trail of broken hearts in our path. We are always on the lookout for new sources of

Fig. 9.18. Multiple Union Lines on Mercury

allurement that feed our mind with excitement. Indeed, without any real sense of commitment, we delight in our infatuation of being with many beautiful, charming, and magnetic individuals. Unfortunately, we may attract like-minded individuals who also lack commitment. So, even though deep down our heart is hungry for affection and thirsty for comforting feelings of love, we end up in relationships that leave us empty, unfulfilled, and drained both physically and emotionally.

✦ HAPPINESS BOOSTER ✦

Grow a Single, Straight Union Line

Selflessly loving and caring for another will grow a Union Line that is singular, deep, and straight, which leads to a happy and contented relationship. A single Marriage Line denotes that our love and affection is focused on one person and that we are committed to that one profound relationship.

The straight line shows that we are fully committed to the relationship and not looking for a way out when things get tough. Despite differences in attitude and opinion, we persist in our partnership until we have created a harmonious union that is smooth and effortless. Because doing this requires us to draw upon our inner reserves of patience, understanding, and forgiveness, developing a straight Union Line makes us a better, stronger, more loving person.

THE BIGGEST HAPPINESS BOOSTER
OF THEM ALL

Choosing Happiness

As we draw toward the conclusion of this book, we want to leave you with a simple message—happiness is a choice. Making that choice enables you to change the lines in your hands for the better, turn happiness blockers into happiness boosters, and create a happier life. We see this in the case of Wayne Dyer, whose choice to be happy not only transformed his life but brought joy to millions of people.

◆◆◆

WAYNE DYER'S STORY
The Wisdom Markings of an Inspirational Giant

Wayne Dyer, EdD, a world-renowned inspirational author, philosopher, and speaker, is a perfect example of how we can transform past hurts and anger into wisdom and empathy, bringing joy and happiness to ourselves and others. We had the privilege of meeting Wayne at different periods in his life. The first consultation was in Florida in 2003; the second was a dozen years later in Ottawa, Canada, in 2015, just a few months before his untimely death. The handprints taken during those readings dramatically illustrate how a shift in perception will inevitably be reflected in changes in our life, in our love, and in our hand.

For many years, happiness eluded Wayne. He grew up in foster homes, spent his youth in poverty, and struggled with depression, issues of self-esteem, and other personal demons. He harbored a deep resentment and hatred for his father, who had abandoned the family early in Wayne's life. Indeed, when he learned that his father had passed away, Wayne drove to his gravesite filled with rage and bitterness. However, during that visit he experienced a life-changing shift in perspective; he suddenly understood that his father had done the best he could. Wayne

Fig. 9.19. Ghanshyam and Wayne Dyer in 2015

said this act of forgiveness released him from a lifetime of anger and pain. In that moment, all the bitterness melted from his heart, changing his life forever. He wrote the book *Your Erroneous Zones*, which became a worldwide bestseller. He stopped drinking and got back into shape. He also started attracting many positive people into his life.

When we first met Wayne and took his handprints in 2003, he had many beautiful wisdom signs, including a Ring of Solomon on his Jupiter mount and a well-formed Love of Truth Line on his Mount of Saturn, reflecting his unwavering spiritual quest for self-awareness.

His print reveals a beautiful, long Heart Line, denoting a deep connection to his feelings and a strong desire to express his love. However, one branch of the Heart Line is turning downward toward the Head Line, reflecting an emotional reservation and a mistrust of others due to past hurt and disillusionment. The long Heart Line reflects a tendency to be deeply disappointed when his love is not returned or when his expectations of others are not met. Wayne confirmed this had indeed been the case with him for a good part of his life—that he had often felt let down in relationships and that his disappointment had disrupted his equilibrium and negatively impacted his personal happiness.

Fig. 9.20. Guylaine taking Wayne's prints in 2003

When we saw Wayne again in 2015, he told us that he had been on a deep spiritual quest to let go of any past hurt and open his heart—he had embraced Vedic philosophy and committed to a daily practice of yoga and meditation. Everything Wayne did was with the deliberate intention to elevate his spirit, deepen his self-awareness, and break down barriers separating himself from others. In other words, Wayne chose to be happy.

We see this in his after handprint where his Heart Line branch is no longer turning downward, confirming that his former emotional reservations had melted away. This reveals his deep conviction to love unconditionally, regardless of how other people treated or responded to him. It also reflects his growing sincerity and willingness to openly share his love and wisdom—both in his relationships and with the world.

The beautiful change of direction, or shift, in Wayne's perception is confirmed by the development of many wisdom markings, including the triple Ring of Solomon on his Jupiter mount, which reflects his profound understanding of human nature and extreme sensitivity to the feelings and problems of others. His Love of Truth Line on Saturn in his before print has turned into a trident, showing he no longer is seeking truth but is living it. He has emerged from the fiery smelting process of Saturn and turned the raw ore of painful life experiences into gold. This is confirmed by the star on his Mount of Sun, which reflects an empathic heart devoted to helping and serving others, as well as a brilliant ability to convey spiritual concepts to the world.

Indeed, Wayne was able to inspire millions and effect positive change in the lives of people around the globe through his books, recorded lectures, and many ongoing philanthropic endeavors, which are now a living legacy of a life dedicated to expressing and sharing love unconditionally.

At the end of his consultation, Ghanshyam told Wayne that the changes in his palms revealed that his heart and his consciousness were moving toward spiritual enlightenment. Wayne smiled and said: "That is my purpose in life—to shift my own consciousness to a more loving and spiritual state, and to help others to do the same. Ghanshyam, you have no idea how happy you've made me today!" He encouraged us to publish his handprints if they could inspire others to open their hearts

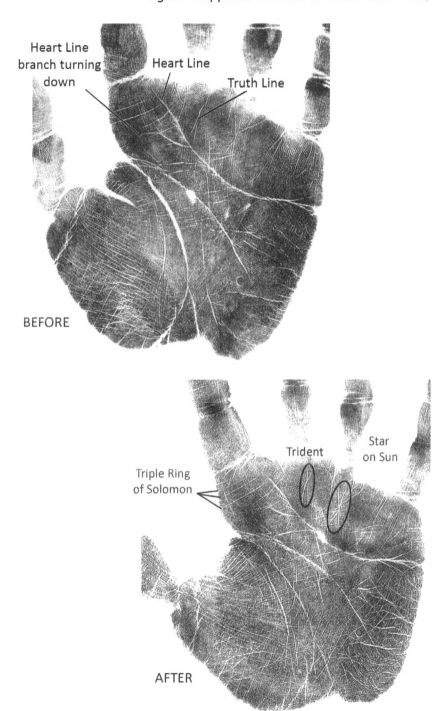

Fig. 9.21. Wayne Dyer's before and after handprints

and find happiness, which, we sincerely hope, they are doing right now as we share them with you. Wayne's last words to us were: "If my prints can help one other person, then share them with the world!"

As Lao-tzu, the father of Taoism, so insightfully mused more than 2,500 years ago: "A journey of a thousand miles must begin with a single step." We have done more than taken that single step—having read this book we are well on our way to a life filled with happiness! It has been our great honor and privilege to have accompanied you on this magnificent journey and to have shared this wonderful adventure with you!

Bibliography

Dispenza, Joe. *Breaking the Habit of Being Yourself: How to Love Your Mind and Create a New One.* Carlsbad, CA: Hay House, 2013.

Harper's Bazaar Staff. "21 of Maya Angelou's Best Quotes to Inspire." *Harper's Bazaar,* May 22, 2017.

Ilibagiza, Immaculée, with Steve Erwin. *Left to Tell: Discovering God Amidst the Rwandan Holocaust.* Carlsbad, CA: Hay House, 2014.

Johari, Harish. *Breath, Mind, and Consciousness.* Rochester, VT: Destiny Books, 1989.

Kuruvilla, Carol. "Amma, the Hugging Saint." *New York Daily News,* July 12, 2013.

Lawrence. *Practicing the Presence of God.* N.p.: Problem Child Press, 2018.

Loyd, Alexander, with Ben Johnson. *The Healing Code.* Illustrated ed. New York: Balance, 2013.

Ortner, Nick. *The Tapping Solution: A Revolutionary System for Stress-Free Living.* 8th ed. Carlsbad, CA: Hay House, 2014.

Paramahansa Yogananda Quotes. Brainy Quote website. BrainyMedia, 2024, accessed July 2, 2024.

Reich, Harold. "A Qualitative Study of Heart-Mind Coherence Techniques for Stress Relief and Mental and Emotional Self-Management." PhD diss., California Institute of Integral Studies, 2009.

Rhoads, Kristoffer. Quoted in McKenna Princing. "This Is Why Deep Breathing Makes You Feel So Chill." Right as Rain by UW Medicine, September 1, 2021.

Teamsoul. "21 Paramahansa Yogananda Quotes to Unveil Your Inner Light." Fearless Soul website, February 4, 2018.

Tolle, Eckhart. *The Power of Now*. Novato, CA: New World Library, 2004.

Vallée, Guylaine. *The Happy Palmist: My Joyful Adventure in Vedic Palmistry*. Chénéville, QC: Galaxy, 2015.

Weissman, Darren. *The Power of Infinite Love & Gratitude: An Evolutionary Journey to Awakening Your Spirit*. Carlsbad, CA: Hay House, 2007.

Yogananda, Paramahansa. *The Divine Romance*. New York: Self-Realization Fellowship Publishers, 1996.

Yogananda, Paramahansa. *How to Cultivate Divine Love*. New York: Self-Realization Fellowship Publishers, 1995.

Index

About the Authors

Ghanshyam Singh Birla (1941–2024)
Founder of the Birla Vedic Center and the Birla Vedic College of Palmistry

Ghanshyam was a world-renowned Vedic palmist-astrologer with more than fifty years of training and experience in Vedic palmistry. Ghanshyam began learning the science of Vedic palmistry and astrology when he was a young boy from his paternal grandfather in India, who was himself a highly respected palmist, astrologer, and Ayurvedic healer. Ghanshyam wrote numerous textbooks on palmistry that are the foundation of the Birla College curriculum including *Luna: The Power of Perception; Venus: The Power of Love; Mars: Your Inner Warrior*; and *Jupiter: The Great Benefic—Tapping into Infinite Possibilities*. He also received an honorary PhD from the Council of Alternative Systems of Medicine, Calcutta, India, in recognition of his work in promoting alternative therapies.

Other Books
by Ghanshyam Singh Birla

Love in the Palm of Your Hand: How to Use Palmistry for Successful Relationships (Destiny Books, 1998)

Magnet Therapy: The Gentle and Effective Way to Balance Body Systems with Colette Hemlin (Healing Arts Press, 1999)
Destiny in the Palm of Your Hand: Creating Your Future through Vedic Palmistry (Destiny Books, 2000)
Introduction to Hast Jyotish: Ancient Eastern System of Palmistry (Galaxy, 2007)

Guylaine Vallée
Vedic Palmist and Astrologer, Teacher, and Media Personality

Guylaine has been practicing Vedic palmistry at the Birla Center since 1985. She has helped thousands of people through her counseling, teaching, and books. In 2015, Guylaine chronicled her life-changing experiences in her biography, *The Happy Palmist: My Joyful Adventure in Vedic Palmistry*. She is also the coauthor, with Kathleen E. Keogh, of *The River of Life: An Unforgettable Journey Within*. Guylaine teamed up with her mentor, Ghanshyam Singh Birla, in 2017 to create and host a series of online 90-Day Challenge programs that illustrate Vedic palmistry's power as a tool for personal self-development.

Online Self-Development Programs
with Guylaine Vallée

The 90-Day Heart Line Challenge: Open Your Heart to Love, Joy and Happiness
The 90-Day Head Line Challenge: Thinking Your Way to Happiness
The 90-Day Life Line Challenge: Experience the Joy of Being Alive
The 90-Day Mounts Challenge: Unleashing the Power of the Planets in Your Hands

Steve Erwin

Biographer, Documentarian,
and Chief Writer for the Birla Center
Steve is a writer and award-winning jour-
nalist who worked in print and broadcast
media for twenty-five years in Canada and
the United States. In New York City, he was
a foreign correspondent for the Canadian
Broadcasting Corporation, reporting on the
9/11 tragedy and its aftermath, as well as a
national news and feature writer for *People* magazine. He has written
seven books, including, with Immaculée Ilibagiza, the *New York Times*
bestselling memoir *Left to Tell: Discovering God Amidst the Rwandan
Holocaust*, which has sold more than a million copies and has been
translated into twenty-five languages. Steve has cowritten *The Happy
Palmist* with Guylaine Vallée and has contributed to all of the Birla
Center publications. He is presently writing the memoirs of Ghanshyam
Singh Birla, who affectionately referred to Steve as Bioji.

For more about the Birla Vedic Center's
programs and services, visit
birla.ca